WOMAN ON TOP

HOW TO WIN
IN A **WOMAN'S WAY**

KAREN A. KOENIG

WOMAN ON TOP
How To Win In A Woman's Way

©2018 Karen Koenig

ISBN-13: 978-1790814206

Publishing and Design:

EPIC AUTHOR
PUBLISHING

Ordering Information: Quantity sales. Special discounts are available on quantity purchases by corporations, associations, and others. For details, contact the publisher at the address above. Orders by U.S. trade bookstores and wholesalers.

Please contact: 800-273-1625 | support@trevorcrane.com | EpicAuthor.com

First Edition

BOOK BONUS

Download your FREE Woman On Top Workbook.

www.WomanOnTop.biz/bonus

This book is dedicated first and foremost to my mother.
She was my role model and mentor until
she died at the young age of 56.

This book is also dedicated to all the women out there
who have endured many of the same struggles I have,
yet who still came out on top.

And finally, to all the men who want to learn how to
help the women they currently work with,
live with and who have yet to be born.

TABLE OF CONTENTS

FOREWARD

BEING EXCELLENT and even well-known in your field just isn't enough nowadays. The internet and the way we work have given us the ability to reach more people than ever. Working and producing results on our own terms but also into a crowded field, where to standout, even though you are a standout, becomes harder each day.

You can be talented and well regarded, but unless you're deliberate about the choices you make, you may not be able to show the world the wisdom that you are here to share, especially for women in a man's world.

Karen Koenig made those deliberate choices each step of the way as she maneuvered herself in three male-dominated industries. First the military, where she reached the rank of Major before she retired, then her position within aerospace where she worked as a team leader, and currently in the financial services where over 80% of representatives are male.

Karen has been battled tested in her journey to success and shares her path, strategies, and stories in how women in male-dominated industries can be truly successful without giving up who they are as women.

Her new book *Woman on Top* gives you the steps and tools for you to be the success you want while being you. Her stories are compelling, and she shares her own journey through these three industries and the common themes that will benefit you as you read this book. It is the right book at the right time for so many of you, as we define what success should be for each of us as women no matter where we are, but especially if the guys outnumber you.

On a personal note, I've been able to walk with Karen as she handled herself, and put into practice, her own strategies as she encountered her own roadblocks that occur when writing a book. She walked her talk, and she shows you that in *Woman on Top*, you can read, learn and implement while being you.

It has been my honor to be a small part of this book's journey and to watch Karen's success with this book.

LoriAnne Reeves, MA
Sales & Business Strategist
Professional Psychotherapist
Speaker & Author

INTRODUCTION

*"The most dangerous phrase in language is:
We've always done it this way."*
—Rear Admiral Grace Hopper

U P UNTIL THE LAST FEW DECADES, business was predominantly male-led. However, that's changing. A recent report *The State of Women Owned Businesses*[1], notes that as of 2016, it is estimated that there are now just over 11.3 million women-owned businesses in the United States, employing nearly nine million people and generating over $1.6 trillion in revenues.

With such a shift occurring in the marketplace, it is hard to believe the story I am about to share with you is true, but it is. I lived it and more ridiculous moments of being disrespected as well, that I will recount to you as you read through the chapters of this book.

But these marketplace shifts also mean I get to choose who I work with today. I like working with people who are open to taking advice. They value what I do. And I want to bring them on as clients because I truly want to help them get results. My niche is women business owners.

When I began working for myself, I determined to focus on women business owners who:

- Have success but still don't feel successful enough

- Spend a lot of time and energy on promoting their business but don't capture or convert enough leads

- Work way too hard for way too little return

- Want to make a change but don't know how

- Feel they need to be perfect before they start

In addition to my stories, I am also going to take you back in time through another portal, and this one leads to the history of all women. I think it will benefit you to read that as we continue to pick up the mantle in this legacy fight, we have to also remember the women who came before us, and who fought for everything we have gained today.

I hope you will enjoy this trip down our sisters' memory lane and you will come away with a renewed purpose to live your life for yourself and for the women who aren't in existence yet.

But before we dive in too deeply, I will start with my experiences of what it's been like to be a woman working in male-dominated fields. There's an old saying that pain is a teacher, and this is the reason we need to tell each other our stories, so we can learn before we lead.

In my previous aerospace job, I was working in the productions systems area. We would take the best processes and procedures from each production system, to design the next best production system for the next generation of aircraft. The theory behind this process was to build planes in less time, with better parts and fewer people. They would be cheaper, faster, and more efficient. However, the reality was we would dig into a portion of the production system, but we were not improving it. It's not that the system was bad; it just needed more technology behind it like robotics. The reason why the company had never explored robotics before was the theory it would get rid of jobs. But really all it was going to do was re-characterize mechanic's jobs; they would learn how to run robotics rather than *being* the robotic.

In regard to robotics, the biggest mind shift was getting the HR department and people in charge of the job codes to consider change. All they needed to do was rewrite job codes and/or they needed to reposition the mechanics to different jobs, as opposed to laying them off. During this time and while we were trying to work this all out, I was constantly told, *"What you're proposing can't be done. We've tried it before, and it didn't work. Besides, this is how we have always done it."* Nothing gets me more driven than to prove these statements wrong. It's not that it couldn't be done; they just didn't want to try, so I challenged their assumptions. I wanted to prove to them they could use a previous method that hadn't worked before because times had changed, and technology was different.

My job was to take the best of the best and improve processes, but no one would listen. Even after we ran the statistics and showed the solution, the people who could have implemented the change still didn't listen. Their mindset was like this: it is easier to hire someone new and train them than to keep them and re-train them into a new area of expertise.

PROCESS IS IMPORTANT. BUT NOT AT THE PRICE OF PEOPLE.

People are the most important assets in any industry. When I was a manager, I would sit down with employees, show them the bottom dollar, and inform them of how they fit into the big picture. I would provide examples of how they were contributing, so they would understand their significance. As I explained this to my employees at the onset, they would often say, *"Oh my gosh, you're the first manager who has taken the time to show us how we fit in!"* My male counterparts didn't take the time to do this as they were worried about getting the work done in the fastest manner possible. This difference in the way women manager and male managers operated seemed to be the most significant to me.

Treating people like people on an emotional level and having an actual relationship with them was key. If you explained what they needed to know in a nice way, people were more apt to work hard for you; this approach was more inclusive and collaborative versus being authoritarian.

I didn't have fears or apprehensions on any project. I did my homework, ran the numbers and went in with the facts. In my experience, men appreciated being presented with numbers and facts. However, my biggest frustration was that I would present the idea to my immediate boss, and then my boss wouldn't necessarily like the idea. Still, he would present it to upper management and lo and behold *they* would like the idea. My boss would never let me present to senior staff, even though I was the one with the idea. So, the rundown was this: He would say it wouldn't work; he would present it anyway, and upper management would like it! This happened time and time again throughout my career.

In the end, I got tired of working for a boss younger than me, who didn't know how to manage people. My staff would present ideas to him, and he would nitpick little details, and then my employees would come to me and gripe about him. I always felt like I was in the middle. Instead of addressing my staff himself, he would tell me, *"Go back and tell them this."* It was silly and immature.

The deciding factor to leave came when for the first time ever, management was given a bonus versus being paid for extra days at the end of the year. That year, my boss gave me the worst performance score I had ever received the entire time I'd worked there. The performance score decided your bonus and I got screwed out of $6,000! When I asked why I'd received such a low score, he said, *"You are a 6-year project manager going up against 20-year manager(s)."*

Again, the human element was not important to him. He wanted to demonstrate a lower number for me because that fit into the curve. He didn't go to bat for me with the skill team to prove I was doing quality work and deserved a high score. It was just a numbers game and black and white management.

Rather than trying to win in a man's world as I attempted to do at that job, I strove to work in a way where I would be commissioned on the results I provided.

My brainstorm baby was, to *"WIN,"* but in a woman's way.

And I wanted the same thing for every other woman out there. I think that's why we create our own worlds as women. There are more women entrepreneurs than men because we are okay with taking on work that may not give us much money the first few years. It offsets the want and need for flexibility.

Some companies say they are family oriented and flexible around your family schedule, but they really aren't. For example, when I was working at my aerospace job, my daughter got sick with depression. She had to go to outpatient therapy at nine in the morning. My schedule was 6-3pm. I asked for the ability to work remotely the first few hours, so I could take her at 9am and then drive into work and finish my day. I wanted flexibility. There wasn't a written policy stating I couldn't work my hours in this way, but the boss said no regardless. His belief was "butts needed to be in seats" for my team and me to be effective.

I chose to use my vacation time instead, even though I shouldn't have had to, as my daughter had priority. In my boss' case, he was young, married, and his wife was a stay-at-home mom. If what happened to my daughter happened to one of his kids, his wife was available. I was divorced and a single parent, and I felt very limited by the nine to five mentality and not being able to be flexible with my schedule to accommodate my family.

And I work with many women who are struggling to balance the same priorities.

Recently, a client of mine bought into and opened up an insurance agency. We sat down, and I talked with her, as we went through everything in her financial background. I asked her what her frustrations, challenges, and concerns were.

She had just set up an office in Stanwood, which is about a 1.5-hour drive in traffic from where she lives. She had come from 23 years in HR and thought she needed to start a business. She also had a side business selling quilting fabric online. When we spoke, she proceeded to tell me she was so stressed out and tired and really didn't want to work with people who needed insurance, because they were becoming very challenging.

I asked her, *"If you could wave a magic wand, what would your ultimate future look like?"* She stated she wanted to retire and put more effort into her fabric business, but she didn't think she could.

I said, *"If I could show you a way to get what you want, would you do business with me?"* She was skeptical that she didn't have to work a nine to five job. However, I showed her she didn't need the insurance business: She lived in one city and had set up the insurance agency in another. The expenses were outweighing the benefits, i.e., wear and tear on her car, gas, new clothes, and food—since she was eating out more often due to time always being crunched. She had no idea what income she was producing off that business, too. Yet her side business, which she loved, selling quilting fabric online, produced $25-35K per year.

I ran the numbers and at our second appointment, said, *"The biggest thing I can show you is that you and your partner can retire today."* Her finances were in great shape; her husband had a solid job, and they were not big spenders. In the end, she sold her business and now does what she loves!

I ask all my clients, *"If you could wave a magic wand, what would your life look like in five or 10 years?"* I encourage them to think and dream again.

So, if you want to:

- Do what you love
- Spend more time with family and friends
- Enjoy life's pleasures such as having your dream car and home

Then, this book is perfect for you.

In this book, you will learn how to:

- Clarify your goals so clearly you can no longer ignore them or stay stuck
- Do what you want in life guilt-free!
- Work with money to achieve any goal you want
- Overcome your fears of failing, being judged, or ridiculed
- Dissolve "perfection-paralysis"

What's the best way to use this book? Read it! I want you to actually read it, enjoy it, and then take away valuable action steps from it that you can use to change your life. Learn from the lessons I'll share inside these pages, so you can be a "Woman on Top" and "Win in a Woman's Way."

At the end of each chapter is also a, "call to action." My challenge to you is to actually take the time to complete each action and transform your life into one you love!

BOOK BONUS:

Book your FREE Discovery call with me, so I can help you drill down into exactly what you need to do to start your business or keep it running in top shape.

Schedule your FREE Discovery Call: www.WomanOnTop.biz/apply

CHAPTER 1:

You Don't Need A Penis To Succeed

"I love to see a young girl go out and grab the world by the lapels. Life's a bitch. You've got to go out and kick ass."
—Maya Angelou

I
T WAS 1987 WHEN I JOINED THE MILITARY with the ultimate goal of becoming a commissioned officer, and it took me 13 years to reach that goal. There were trials and failures along the way and a lot of lessons learned. That experience is what propelled me to write this book and share with you my journey through three career moves in male-dominated industries.

I was stationed at a base that had posted for a new commissioned position. I knew I wanted to apply and that I could lead. However, a male commanding officer had other ideas about me and didn't feel I was officer material. Unfortunately, he made that known. I'd had a run-in with him earlier in my enlisted career, and he didn't care for me. A friend of mine, who was also a woman, happened to be the chair of the selection process and she knew I was right for the commissioned position. Usually, when an officer was selected from the enlisted ranks, the board was made up of peers. There were basic questions used to interview the person, and a deliberation process ensued on who should be considered for the commission. To legitimize this process, so there were no doubts, she made sure there was a scoring matrix used during the hiring process. She also made sure the selection board was made up of a cross selection of people from the base who didn't know me. This ensured the process was fair and the right candidate (which happened to be me) would be the best fit for the position. I received my commission in 2000, a few months before my 35th birthday.

I made it to the rank of major and commanded at two different times in my military career, one in Services Flight and the other in Communications Flight. My desire to be in the military was lifelong. From the time I was a child, I wanted to honor my mom and follow in her career as a military officer. She was the first woman succeeding in a man's world that I had ever seen or heard of. It was her example that helped me reach my goals.

My parents both served their country in the military. Mom was an officer and a nurse while Dad enlisted and served as an Emergency Medical Technician (EMT). They met in the military in the late 1950s when the Armed Forces were very different. Women were not allowed in field positions. They could only serve in administration or nursing roles and had to get out of the military when pregnant.

In fact, in the1930s, just one year after The Great Depression hit it was assumed that women would stay home and raise the children and keep house. Because men were regarded as the primary earners, and the country was in a hard reset with the number of available jobs bottoming, women were paid in the way in which they were perceived…as second-grade earners deserving of second-grade pay.

The beloved Amelia Earhart was still with us through 1937 when she and her navigator, Fred Noonan, and her plane disappeared over the Pacific. Her story is worth noting because she is a female pioneer for the ages.

Also, during the Depression, a woman you may have never heard of, Frances Perkins, became the first woman cabinet official as the Secretary of Labor, appointed by Franklin D, Roosevelt. Add to that the 1938 Supreme Court decision that minimum wage legislation is indeed constitutional, and Perkins paved the way for the "social safety net" that includes unemployment insurance, minimum wage laws and the Social Security system[2]

In the 80s, it felt as though women hadn't made much progress at all…

In 1987, women were allowed in all positions in the military except combat. I became an enlisted, electronic mechanic. Traditionally this wasn't a position that women went into; you had to have high scores on the ASVAB (the military test), to get into this career field. Women continued to gravitate toward administrative and medical professional positions. Even as I was out-processing to go to basic training, my first sergeant tried to sway me into taking an administrative role before I left. Later, I worked with him, and it was a tad awkward knowing how he really perceived me and my skill set. Also, in my experience, the men I was around at the time didn't want women in the military. But I was determined to follow where my strengths lie. Since I'd received high scores in all categories on my test, I chose a specialty that wasn't traditionally picked by women. After graduating from technical school, I was the only female in the shop working with all men. I wanted to fit in, but, that didn't mean I had to compromise my femininity.

I always had my hair fixed nicely, my makeup on and my nails done; whether I was in Battle Dress Uniform (BDUs) or my dress blues, which was a formal uniform. I wouldn't compromise my femininity just to be in uniform, no matter if I was out on the flight line working on aircraft or in the office doing computer work.

At the beginning of my career, I was treated differently because I was a woman, not because I couldn't do the job. On multiple occasions, male counterparts would force me to do strenuous, physical work, which by regulation, were two-person tasks. They did this just to see if I could do the jobs solo and if I would turn them into the supervisor for assigning me work that broke regulation. This was a safety issue, but I would jump in and do the tasks alone, just to prove I could do them without their help.

Sometimes as I was learning, managing men was just… weird.

One instance where I was treated as an inferior, stands out like a bump on the noggin! I was working in the electronics shop when a gentleman said something derogatory and I told him to be quiet. In response, he actually picked up a book and hit me on the head! Of course, I went to my superior, the shop supervisor. He was a very non-confrontational person and brought the two of us together in a room and told the guy who'd hit me to apologize to me. The justification as for why he had hit me over the head wowed me! He said, *"Well, the reason why I treated you like that is because you remind me of my wife."* And I said, *"Oh, so that's how you treat your wife?"*

Not every circumstance was as extreme, but I still fielded challenges frequently, even in my new position.

When I was in charge of the base Honor Guard, an elite group of enlisted members who performed for military ceremonies, I once again leapt into a situation without understanding the outcome. I was asked to do a change of command ceremony. This is where one commander steps down from a position, and a new one comes into the position, whatever that may be. They wanted the Honor Guard in BDUs vs. Dress Blues. I told the requesting officer the Honor Guard was not meant to be in BDUs, and that regulation didn't allow for it. The commanding officer basically told me I needed to do what I was told. I argued, *"Well, how about we contact the Adjutant General and explain the situation? It will look good to have the Honor Guard in dress blues. It will offset everyone else being in BDUs, and more than likely he doesn't realize we don't have an Honor Guard BDU uniform we can perform in."* The commanding officer continued to tell me to do it the way I was told. I responded, *"In that case, you will have to find someone else to do it other than the base Honor Guard because I am not going to go against the regulation."* I felt he was pushing me around because I was a woman and I don't like being made to do something that isn't right. I knew what the regulations were, and I had attended training for this particular regulation. I was in charge of the base Honor Guard, and so I had been specifically trained to know this regulation backward and forward.

Later, I was coached by a Chief Master Sergeant—the highest enlisted rank—about my tendency to jump into assignments without first thinking of the consequences. It wasn't the best way to approach situations in the military, and at first, I have to admit I was defensive. He was trying to let me know I needed to think before I acted; a good lesson that I have never forgotten. I probably shouldn't have done two-person tasks just to prove I could, and I should have respected the officer who asked me to provide an Honor Guard for a change of command ceremony. In battle, acting before thinking can be useful, but with people and situations, you must weigh what's going on.

In the end, I realized I had to take it all in stride. As an officer, all I could do was provide advice and guidance. I could give advice on how to solve a situation and guide the person to the best solution. As I learned, I adjusted my approach and came to realize it was okay if my recommendation wasn't taken. I had said my peace and offered the best solution I could. Whether they chose to accept it or not was their decision.

Advice and guidance was the best solution, and I could see when I applied it, it did work—especially when I was deployed to a Navy Air Station in Diego Garcia as Services Commander. The previous commander had found that the Navy was buying bottled water and charging triple the price to the Air Force. She'd handed the issue over to me prior to leaving. I then presented the issue to the Air Force base commander and gave the facts. He asked me for a solution. I advised that the Air Force should stop buying bottled water from the Navy and guided him to the solution, which was to order refillable water bottles. I presented the facts and the solution and allowed him to make the choice. He chose to accept my solution. We ended up saving the government tons of money.

Before I retired completely from the military, I was hired into the defense side of the aerospace industry, another completely male-dominated field. I felt at home; as they valued the military experience I brought to the table. I was hired in as a first-line manager, and as ironic as it sounds, managed a crew of all men. Instead of being in an all-male shop and being the only female worker, here I was the only female manager leading a crew of all men. What I found was managing men was way easier than being managed by men.

I oversaw technicians whose job was maintenance and technical troubleshooting of electronic and mechanical equipment on the ground or via fixed towers. It was a hot, arid, sandy environment and we worked out of a mobile trailer while the permanent building was being built for that division. I was told by my manager that I needed to dress the part of a first-line manager. For that company, it meant wearing business attire.

I spent a good majority of my time outdoors or walking between the mobile trailer and the maintenance building where we did our work on equipment. You can't wear shoes with any type of heel in the sand, and business attire is not practical in 110-degree weather either. I proceeded to wear practical shoes and business casual attire while at the site. When I was visited by upper-management or was off-site, I wore the business attire I was told to wear.

When I transferred from the Desert Southwest to the green and lush Pacific Northwest for this company, I observed an interesting anomaly with the women who worked in the commercial aircraft division. This job was entirely indoors, in an open factory. Most women dressed casually in khaki pants, dress-shirts, comfortable shoes, and very little makeup. This really was the environment to wear business attire, and it didn't seem to be the norm based on what I had observed. When asked, these women told me it was the way to get ahead in the industry, i.e., to look more like the men. But, I did the total opposite; I had long hair, wore makeup, dressed in slacks and nice blouses, and wore dressy shoes, which was considered business attire. I was just as successful or more so because I refused to deter from my femininity simply because I worked in another male-dominated field. I felt good about myself, and I believe this helped me excel in my career.

While it may seem like dressing to honor your individuality and comfort is a small statement, I think this decision allowed me to stand out from the other women who were trying to blend in with their male counterparts. The men wore business dress, and the women felt that to join their network and to be seen as a strong worker they needed to dress similarly to the men. No jewelry, or makeup. No nails. If I was told that a reasonable and modest blouse was "too provocative" I wore it anyway. When I was working in Arizona, our dress code was decided by superiors in another state. I was told to wear business attire even when I was out tromping in between buildings in the sand. But I was not going to wear heels and a dress in that climate. Knowing where to plant my flags and which battles to engage in has made all the difference, and I have been able to keep my integrity—which is the most important objective of all.

I learned the hard way; it didn't matter if I was a successful first-line manager and that people thrived under my leadership. I realized this when I wasn't selected as the second-line manager to fill in while the previous manager was out on family leave. An older third-line manager didn't think I knew enough about the aircraft to lead the division, because I hadn't "earned" my way there. In the end, he put a male counterpart into the position at the last minute, without so much as a conversation with me.

I observed the gender of the people who were and weren't promoted and tried to tie in together the common elements of why a co-worker would be granted permission to ascend the ladder of success. I noted the one female second-level manager had come up through the ranks by working on the aircraft. In contrast, I had a military aerospace background. I tried to follow this female manager's lead and that of the two other women who were also promoted.

It was a time of hope for me until I learned my work history and background were not respected and that a male co-worker set me straight. This co-worker didn't have a degree, but he told me that if he were up for the position, he wouldn't lose any sleep over it. He knew he would get it, and confided, *"In part, because I am a man."*

As a woman, that was a tough industry to crack, and I know I am not the only gal on the line who felt this way. This was my reality, and it is still the reality of so many women in every sector of every industry.

Today I work in another male-dominated industry, financial services, where the majority of women hold administrative jobs. As odd as it seems, 30 years later since I have been out of the military where 95% of women held analyst positions, I still see the same types of behaviors. In this industry, we are instructed to wear professional attire, which mainly consists of suits and collared shirts for men, and dresses and pantsuits for women. Some of the new, younger women try to emulate men in their dress by wearing black suits, collared shirts, and minimal makeup. During a training session, we were instructed via a skit by two white men on how to properly dress the part of an advisor. I know what professional attire is; I know how to dress according to my body type and style, and I'm not going to set aside my femininity, so that I can look like everyone else.

The other observation I have made in the financial industry is that female financial advisors are treated differently than the male advisors. The male advisors are asked to be in leadership positions sooner, and at training events, 95-100% of the presenters are male. Women represent 36% of the region I am in, but very few are asked to be in leadership positions. In the last three years, I have only seen a total of 4-5 women present at training events.

But I don't want to come across as anti-men or as a woman basher. I believe women can learn just as much from men as men can from us. For example, men will apply for new jobs with only 60-65% experience, whereas women think they need to be 100% proficient. Men set their goals and strive to meet them no matter what anyone else says, and women tend to change their aims based on feedback from family and friends. In these cases, women can definitely learn from men how to be more assertive and confident without compromising their original aspirations.

In the end, you can learn from men. I learned to think before I acted on something. I learned to stick to what I knew was right and to use advice and guidance as a tool to provide answers. I learned I preferred to lead men rather than to be led by men. I learned it might've been easier to work my way up to a leadership role, but leading takes more than knowledge. It takes knowing and understanding people. And finally, I learned you could be a successful woman in male-dominated industries, without emulating masculine behavior and without sacrificing your femininity and grace.

IN YOUR JOURNAL:

Answer the following questions:

- Look at your life and compare what you do, versus what you would prefer to do. What would you do if you could be uncompromisingly who you want to be?

- Where in your life are you executing processes a certain way, even though you know there is a better way, but you aren't being listened to when you make suggestions?

- Where in your life are you doing work for someone else, but it's not congruent with who you are?

Once you've answered those questions, review the next section carefully to give you the energy and enthusiasm to succeed in reaching your own goals. Take a look at the following women who are winning in male-dominated fields.

Why do I share this with you? Because you can do this, too! Your name can be included in a book maybe even in the next year if you get laser-focused on your goals. Sometimes, before we believe we can succeed at whatever we put our mind to, we need to learn about other people who have blazed a trail before us.

THROUGH MY INTERVIEWS, I MET THESE OUTSTANDING WOMEN WHO ARE SHINING ROLE MODELS FOR EVERY WOMAN:

Heather Lewis, hit a six-figure commission in year two of working in the financial industry, and a seven-figure commission after eight years. Her biggest triumph is that she dominates in a male-centric industry and persists in the face of adversity.

Dawn Jones brought in six figures with her safety training company in three years, after conquering major hurdles in building her business such as finding clients and reworking her business model.

Julia Hansberry is renown in her network marketing company. This industry employs over 70% of women, but the people who are making the most money are men. As a woman, she is a standout and an example to keep working to attain what you want most.

BOOK BONUS:

Go to www.WomanOnTop.biz/bonus to help you plot out your success to WIN in a male-dominated world.

CHAPTER 2:

Why Getting Ready To Be Ready Doesn't Work

---

*"If we wait until we are ready, we'll be waiting
for the rest of our lives."*
—Author Unknown

I ONCE WORKED WITH A FEMALE COLLEAGUE who was stuck at being 100% proficient at something before making a start. She wanted to move from project management into finance. Gains: she would have been paid more; she wasn't happy in project management; she would have been happier in finance.

But, instead of making the move, she devalued her ability because she felt she needed to know 100% how to do the job she was applying for. She didn't believe in her current ability, or that she could add to the area in which she wanted to work, because she thought she needed to know a lot about finance or that she had to have a finance background.

As a result, she missed out on applying for a perfect job. In hindsight, she realized all she had to do in that role was populate spreadsheets and keep numbers in order, which she could already do! But she thought she needed a degree in finance. Essentially, she could have taken her project management skills and applied them to finance to find the success she wanted anyway!

This is something I've never understood, and perhaps to my detriment, but in my life, I have never felt the need to be 100% proficient. I am not sure why I am like this, but if I want something I go after it and internally say, *I can learn what I don't know, or I can acquire the skill I need for a job.*

Women's need for job validation came about as more women entered the workforce in the 1940s. Remember Rosie the Riveter? It was WWII, and the men were deployed and fighting, leaving the women responsible to hold down the fort and carry on business. Before the men left in droves to fight for our country, women had held primarily nursing, secretarial or caregiving jobs. Women were interestingly enough described as "still feminine under the dirt." To take a peek at what that turn of phrase translated into as far as the dress women wore, I invite you to Google some of the stunning real-life images of women from that era working on everything from fixing airplanes to undertaking assembly line work.

DO FIRST. THINK LATER. LEARN BY DOING.

That's been my motto. When I was a kid; I wanted to learn how to ride a bike. But, I am stubborn and didn't want anyone to help me. So, my brother said I should just straddle the bike at the top of a hill, lift my feet up, and then I would coast down the hill...all I had to do was balance. Well, I believed him! Little did I know that if I started at the top of a hill, I would be going very fast by the time I got to the bottom.

Also, I didn't know how to brake, nor did I ask. By the way, I was riding a bike that had a braking system that was controlled by reversing the pedals…of which my feet were NOT on because I had lifted them and let the pedals spin! By the time I got to the bottom, I was screaming at my brother, *"How do I stop?!?!"* And, low and behold, I hit a lifted piece of sidewalk and wiped out. I ended up cracking my head on the cement and getting a big goose egg, but you know what? I learned how to ride a bike! I did it first, thought about consequences later, and then I learned how to do it better.

PERFECTION IS NOT PROGRESS.

Perfection is defined as everything is or has to be, 100% accurate or in place. Perfection paralysis is when everything has to be 100% to move forward, where progress should be going from 50 to 60%… If you are improving, that is progress. The primary focus is starting somewhere and improving on where you are, which is better than not starting at all. Everything is learnable. When people think they need to be perfect, they often don't get started at all.

Now don't get me wrong, I don't recommend that women try to repeat what I did with a bike. Taking physical risks is different than taking emotional risks. Most women who want to change, are often not taking physical risks, but they are stuck in the *fear* of what might happen if they aren't perfect before they start.

They fear they are a fraud and that they will get "caught."

They fear they cannot apply for other jobs.

They fear ridicule from peers.

But these are irrational fears.

I still hear from women today: *"I need a finance degree to work as a financial advisor,"* or *"I need to know something about investing."* Had that been me, I wouldn't be an advisor today as I didn't have either. You have to be good with people, and you have to build relationships. All the rest you can learn as you go. To move forward, you have to reverse engineer the skillset. When you apply this thinking, you can *shift* your fears about the situation.

When I was in aerospace, a lot of millennial women worked for me. I found that these women thought they must be 100% good at their skills before they went after a new job. Alternatively, the millennial men didn't even think about proficiency and knew only about 60-65% about that new job. But that didn't stop them. They would go in and apply for that new job anyway. You don't have to be 100% proficient, or 100% accurate. You are just as smart as everyone else. I was trying to teach these girls to get their brain out of the way. The six inches between your ears can be your worst enemy.

The first step to overcome perfection syndrome is to evaluate what skills you have and to write them all down. What could taking that *first step* look like in the context of your business, career, personal relationships, family, etc.?

First, believe in your abilities in each of these areas. You may have a skill you learned being a stay-at-home mom (SAHM) that you could apply to a potential position. It's all about how you look at what you can bring to a position. Let's look at what skills a stay-at-home mom might apply to a job outside the home.

SAHMs:

- Know how to do a budget.
- Are organized with their time.
- Have emotional regulation and are cool under pressure.

- Know how to work with people of different personalities. You could have two or three kids with different personalities, for instance.

- Know client care: Only these clients (their children) can't be fired no matter what! They will be their children for life!

For example, I have emotional regulation, and I am cool under pressure. Back when my daughter was eight, she fell while riding a scooter and split her kneecap. I had just gotten done making dinner and to keep the calm, I told her *"Hey, let's eat,"* and then I put ice on her knee. After dinner, I cleaned up the dishes and then announced we needed to go to the emergency room. She and my son asked, *"Why?"* I calmly stated that I knew the knee needed stitches and it always takes so long in the waiting room, that I wanted to make sure she and her brother had been fed before we went. Once she understood, she was fine with it.

The next step is to extrapolate the skills you wrote down to fit the job you want to apply for. Change these for each type of job.

For example, starting your own business calls for these skills:

- Good with working on an island and by yourself.
- Focused on bringing in clients.
- Understanding the value of time.
- Figuring out what you're not good at and delegating the rest. If you aren't good at computer stuff, you must hire someone. If you aren't good at marketing, then hire someone to do that for you. Even if it is exciting, but it's not your strength, it's not worth your time or money.

Now, the next step is to look at what makes you happy out of the skills you possess and look for a career or job that takes all your skills into consideration. Don't compromise a family/life balance. Figure out what makes you happy and what you enjoy.

Remember the client of mine who was in the fabric business, who was at odds over her insurance business? While we were sitting there, she came up with ideas to make more money for her fabric business. For example, instead *of selling* unique fabrics. She made quilting kits, so the fabric is already cut for the quilts you want to make. Then she put everything a person needs to make a quilt in a kit and sold it. Some people would buy the kit, while others liked to cut the little tiny squares. The thinking is *if someone cuts this shit for me I can make the quilt!*

YOUR TO DO:

1. Think of something you wanted to act on in your life. It's important to you. Your why.
2. Reflect on what you think you must know or have in place before you start.
3. Assume that isn't true.
4. Take a log of your existing skill set and find the job or business that fits it.
5. Make that change.

In reference to the list above, can you recall a goal that you've filed away in the back of your head? Something that you greatly want to achieve but you have held back from getting started because you felt you needed to be overprepared? This is the time to embrace taking those first steps to make your aim a reality. See how it feels to simply take action and worry about the imperfections that pop up later.

No matter how prepared we are (or think we are) to embark on our goals, the timing is never perfect. You will still have surprising developments that you didn't anticipate and that you will need to resolve. You will still have to, at points, deviate from your Plan A and use your Plan B. Why not make this the year that you leap with all the passion in your heart to accomplish what you have been dreaming about?

AN INTERVIEW WITH KAREN WHITTIER

When I interviewed one woman, Karen Whittier, this is what she shared with me about feeling as though she needed to have everything in her life perfect before she could move forward in the profession that she wanted to work in. In her words:

"I wish I would have just gone ahead with going into what I feel so passionate about."

Take a lesson from her and focus on your passions. Dedicate to yourself that you will find a way to both work in your passion and monetize it.

Karen started out as an engineer in the 1970s because her dad told her that she needed to go into something that would pay the bills. But this was not her passion at all, and instead, she started a farm preschool. After getting her hard-won dream over the finish line, she, unfortunately, had to sell out her portion due to arthritis. Today, she makes activity cards for kids; the cards have barcodes on them, and you can use a website that goes along with them to access additional family activities to download.

Despite her driving urge to make it in a man's world, Karen definitely had her setbacks that she had to deal with and overcome. If she didn't, she would have let antiquated attitudes about women's rights and fair treatment take over, and she wouldn't have made it as far in her career as she has.

The reality of how women engineers were perceived was like a bucket of cold water thrown on Karen, who worked for a male boss.

"My boss, every time I would walk into the office to either try to get an assignment or even check on something…would never talk about work."

Karen's boss, instead, liked to talk about what his kids were doing, particularly, his son who was her age. He asked her repeatedly if she was interested in dating him. As you can expect, Karen's reaction was: *"It was just so uncomfortable and very awkward."*

But not all men treated her as though her presence was a challenge. She worked with a thoughtful man who had worked his way up from blue-collar positions into management. Once he gave Karen a tip that she has never forgotten and for which she remains grateful.

When she remembers the kindness of this man, she says, *"If a guy was a good guy, he was a good guy. Whether he was blue collar or white collar."*

Karen had come into work one day dressed in business attire and then had to do an inspection that required her to climb a ladder. Well, she hadn't planned that far ahead in her day, or even thought about the consequences of her attire, and she had worn a skirt.

This gentleman said, *"Karen, I just want you to know, um, when you go out into the mill, you need to change into some overalls or something."*

She looked at this man astounded that she had been so oblivious as to climb a ladder in a skirt above a floor of men. Saying, *"Are you kidding me?"* It had simply never occurred to her what their viewpoint was but thank goodness he had informed her of what was going on.

Another time she was in a huge meeting with collars of all colors when a man grabbed ahold of her rear end. She, in turn, grabbed ahold of his wrist and took it off her body. Then she ordered him in a loud, stern voice: *"Don't touch me. Keep your hands off me."* No one else in the room had anything to say about it, and the meeting went on.

Because of what transpired later, Karen believes her boss must've contacted the guilty party. A couple of days later she was supposed to receive reports, and other documents, but whatever had been planned for her suddenly halted.

"It was a double-edged sword," she states, *"If you caused waves there will always be repercussions."*

The incidents didn't end there. Karen often found anonymous pieces of paper with naked bodies on them laid on her desk. She had to hear comments from men wondering what size her breasts were, and what kind of man would marry her since she was so obviously gay having taken over a "man's job," one that this imaginary man could use to feed his family.

"I would come home crying night after night. It was just such a horrible, horrible, horrible environment."

But she hung in there and refused to quit for a couple of reasons. Her family had sent her to college, and she felt tremendous gratitude for the sacrifices they had made to allow that to happen. Second, she always had a crazy notion that she owed the women's movement a debt. She thought if she didn't put up with the abuse at work that the movement would be set back decades—kind of like paying her dues to keep the progress rolling along.

Legally, she didn't find the support that she needed to help her mediate the situation, so she elected to put up with the hostile environment until she could get out.

As a result, she learned that if she could go back in time, she would have readily immersed herself into her passions. "I wouldn't have worried about being able to support myself. I would've just gone straight into teaching no matter what

Now, Karen advocates that women should help them find their way back to doing what they love. For her, that meant reestablishing her personal freedom. And she found this renewed liberation through yoga. Yoga centered her and allowed her to get back to being an advocate for children. That's when she turned her energy toward promoting learning through play for children and established her farm preschool. It is still her belief that: *"Too many children nowadays do not have enough time or access and freedom to play. That is the way they learn best. My passion is to help bring more play to children and to support parents to facilitate that at their homes."*

"I'm engineering education," she says. *"I will say that I do want to make money, but that's not my driving force. When people are passionate about what they are doing, the money follows."*

Before Karen switched her focus to her learning cards, the children on her farm were treated to the privilege of playing with the animals out in the yard, but she also brought other animals into the classroom, so the kids could interact with them. On the weekend, families engaged on a deeper level with her animals that she remembers fondly.

"Maybe the family didn't have a pet at home, and they weren't necessarily sure they wanted to commit to a full-time pet. But they could commit to having a pet for a weekend."

The kids loved it, and Karen continues to love them and her job, too.

NOW YOU:

After reading Karen's story, ask yourself:

Am I working in the right field?

Am I going to have regrets later because I didn't choose a heart-centered business?

BOOK BONUS:

Please connect and share your personal story of what you have dealt with and overcome in the workplace. Let's support each other in our special sisterhood!

I can help you navigate current problems and assist you in developing a plan to keep moving forward in your career as you overcome them. Share your story with me here: www.WomanOnTop.biz/apply

CHAPTER 3:

Success Doesn't Mean You Self-Sacrifice Self-Care

"A successful woman is one who can build a firm foundation with the bricks others have thrown at her."
—Author Unknown

IN THE 1950s, newer fields for women are rising to the surface. More women are taking on jobs in engineering, pharmacy, real estate, and finance. This is the era of announcing the intention to attain professional equality. Also, in this decade, stewardesses were called "sky girls," and increased numbers of women chose real estate as their profession. Apparently, real estate is a natural and logical choice for women due to their "homemaking interests."

We all know women often feel guilty when they do something for themselves instead of taking care of others first, which is why we had the lock on caregiving occupations until we started using our voice to make different career decisions.

It is important to have *fun* at what you do. If you have fun at what you are doing, you are more productive, happy, and you tend to attract like-minded people. You want to surround yourself with people you want to be, or you want to emulate their behavior. You also want to love your work! This is important, and work is so much more than a means to an end. Work can be a joy. It can be an outlet. It can be a source of pride and excitement. The work you choose can stoke the fire of your hunger for knowledge or shut it down completely because the drudgery is so wearing on you.

After I got divorced, in 2008, I was in between jobs.

I was living in Arizona as a stay-at-home mom. I was still in the Air Force reserves, so I had some reserve pay coming, and I was completing my MBA at the same time. Due to all of these circumstances, I was making very little money, gas was $4 per gallon for diesel, and I couldn't really afford to feed the kids.

Because of the divorce, the kids were going back and forth between houses every week. One particular week they came back from being at their dad's house, and asked me when they could go on vacation with me. Apparently, they had recently been camping with their dad, and I felt guilty that I couldn't take them on vacation, as I could barely afford to put gas in my car.

I explained to them they had just had a vacation with their dad, so perhaps we could do a staycation; hanging at home and binge-watching movies and eating popcorn. We could also plan play dates at the park with friends and do other inexpensive activities.

When we first got divorced, we both earned enough not to get child support money from the other. But since then I had been laid off from my job, and I had enough money just for the necessities, but I didn't have money to buy food. It didn't even occur to me to take care of my own needs, and I didn't even feel I had the right to ask for support, and for what I wanted.

I had the fear that my ex-husband wouldn't help out since our divorce decree stated no child support. And I was sure he would make me go back to court to change the decree if I asked him for any money. Actually, asking him took me months! I ran scenarios through my head about what he would say. I didn't even put gas in my car or drive places because I got so low on cash. I was working a couple of jobs from home in project management. One was for a business website developer in Hawaii, and the other was for a publishing business in South Carolina. Even though I was working, I just didn't have enough money at the end of the month to feed my kids when they were at my house.

I felt bad. I was afraid. The divorce was ugly. My ex-husband was a stickler about the amount of time we split between the kids. There are an odd number of days in the year, but we HAD to make sure it was half and half. Anytime we switched weekends; he made me put it in writing. He wasn't very flexible about the entire process.

I finally got up the courage to ask for a mere $500 per month to supplement my income, so I could feed the kids while they were at my house. After talking with him, I realized he wanted to make sure our kids were fed, too. And, $500 a month was not a lot for food for two growing kids. In the end, he cordially agreed and genuinely felt bad that I was in such a position. It was to my delight; I learned that he understood. I had more internal angst about the entire situation, and I wasted a lot of time because I was basing what I thought his reaction would be off his previous behavior. It took me too long to get the nerve to even ask him because I wanted to make sure he would say yes.

In this instance, I had emotional turmoil; I wasn't giving 100% to the two people I was a parent to, and I had a lot of guilt because I couldn't do the fun stuff I wanted to with my kids.

The problem was, people got what they needed or wanted at my expense. They didn't understand the turmoil or angst affecting me outside of work, because I didn't articulate what I wanted or needed to those around me. I put 100% into everything that I did, and it wasn't good for me. Eventually, the whole situation resulted in the worst-case scenario for everyone. So, I made a change and switched up the people I spend my time with.

Some of the positive people I choose in my life include:

- The guy I am dating. Date a positive person who is always bettering themselves. He has been divorced twice, so we both wanted something different from what we had come from.

- I am attracted to friends or people who become my friends, who are positive people. My best friend since seventh grade, of 35+ years, is a positive, fun person.

- You can't choose your family, though! I have a few negative members, but I opt not to be around them or feed into their negativity.

If you have kids, ask someone to help with the kids. My friends would watch my kids, and then we would swap, and go do girl stuff. Don't be afraid or loath to ask people for help.

At a breakfast the other day, this woman, who is a therapist, was talking about boundaries, specifically about saying *no* without feeling guilty. For example, she only had certain availabilities for new patients, and this particular new patient could only meet on Mondays. So, the therapist acknowledged if Monday was the only day she could meet, she told her she had availability in six weeks.

The new patient said this was too long in the future, so through more conversation, the therapist offered, *"If you need to meet sooner, I have Thursday at 2pm available, which do you prefer?"* The therapist set her boundary and gave the new patient availability either in six weeks or three days from that moment, and she didn't deviate.

You must know what your limits are. If you know what your schedule is, stick to it and don't deviate, you won't feel guilty about reinforcing boundaries.

I naturally do this in a professional setting. I tell clients my availability, then offer, *"Which time/day works better for you?"* It helps to put the responsibility of making the decision that works for them on the other person.

And there has to be a *fair exchange*. Fair exchange means doing the same for others. For every hour you work, spend 10 minutes on yourself. Get up and do something. You cannot and should not sit and work for four hours. Get up to grab a glass of water and go to the bathroom. Practice self-care within the day as well. I learned this after having my hip surgery. I physically can't sit down for extended periods of time, so I have to get up and walk around.

In the year 2018, self-care is not a suggestion it is a necessity that stretches across all the areas of your life. The definition of success should include the fact that you have made and followed plans to give yourself time to unwind, unplug and relax without pressure.

One woman I heard of in the process of writing this book, defines self-care as calling the repairman to fix her garage door so her family will be safe. She has also noted that buying her comfortable "house shoes" was indicative of self-care. She's got the right idea of flipping the expectations of self-care on their head, so why can't we expand self-care practice into our work? Why shouldn't we include it in our definition of success?

We are living in a time of women striving for more holistic enlightenment. When one woman I interviewed, Julia Hansberry embarked on her first job, she knew she was going to be successful. But before she could shoot for success, she had to know what it meant. Back in the day, self-care was not included in this equation. Julia's traces her magnetism to success to the way she was brought up and the work ethic that was instilled from her father who had an entre-preneurial spirit.

His attitude and choices set him apart from other relatives in her family who she admits were chauvinistic.

From her induction into network marketing at the peak of the housing crisis, she learned that if she were to do it all over again, the first class that women entrepreneurs should take would be the importance of growth and development.

Julia says, *"But what sold me on the profession was the ability to help somebody create life-changing income."*

Why do we not spend time on taking care of ourselves and plan-ning for our business and life goals regularly? Why do not take the time to understand the value of boundaries and how to set them?

These are the guidelines I use for when I need to accept boundaries:

1. Am I unable to control my reactions from this person in my life, and is it harming me or the people around me?
2. Is this a one-sided relationship where I am doing most of the nurturing and making the attempts to stay in contact?
3. Do the people in my life genuinely want the best for me, or do they spend their time talking about my mistakes?
4. Despite my sharing my feelings and what needs to change in the relationship, am I ignored?
5. Am I being blamed for everything that has ever gone "wrong" in the relationship?

It's critical that we carve out time in our lives to defend our right to self-care. Self-care for business women also includes giving your-self the time and resources to keep growing and learning. You want to be known as the expert in your field; every class you take, mentor you speak to, or mastermind you attend, needs to be undertaken with that end goal in mind.

Darren Hardy advises that business owners should set aside 10% of their income to fund their personal growth and development.

Despite the stumbling blocks in her way that so many women are charged with navigating, Julia also knew when she was first married that she would not be a stay-at-home mom. She would be a career girl and would continue to break the mold restraining women. Many years in the same specialty have taught her that women are also responsible for creating ourselves as a product of our environment.

Julia states, *"We have to give ourselves a little more grace."* And we do have to go easier on ourselves. Yes, we have come a long way, but we have so much further to go. She tells me it's interesting to note that in her profession men are the top money earners in the field although there are more women.

Of course, she suffered from working mother's guilt even though her mother and grandmother were both single moms. The fact that she was helping people to save their money by earning a mere $500 did alleviate her guilt a little, but she couldn't deny who she was and what she needed to survive. She tells me her own mother still fights back the guilt over working so much when her kids were little.

Because Julia works in a field that mainly employs women she finds the support she needs in other women who are in the same situation. They defend mommy time and more self-care time…and this includes blocking time to work on their careers, to become the self-made women they've dreamt about since they were little girls. Not only should you schedule time for business and self-care, but if you really want to get a handle on your schedule and organization, then you need to schedule EVERYTHING.

Whatever you don't want to deal with when you get home from work at night, make sure you take the time to complete in the morning. One of Julia's favorite quotes is *"Perfection is the perfect procrastinator."* Take imperfect action instead. This is a much wiser decision than doing nothing or caving in to being frozen in indecision.

Self-care is one of the most vital changes that women need to get behind making. We are still responsible for our futures and our presents after all.

YOUR TO DO:

- What two actions can you take in the next week to make sure you are doing self-care?
- Write down two things that make you happy.
- Practice setting boundaries. When you set boundaries, you have more time to honor your need for self-care and to do what makes you happy.

YOUR TO DO FOR MY SELF-CARE:

Please review my book. Did you know that every review you leave makes a difference? Your review could also help other women who might need this book, so you'd be paying it forward. You can leave your review here: www.WomanOnTop.biz/review

Thank you for your support, sister!

CHAPTER 4:

Finding The Truth And Asking For Help

"Once you realize you deserve better, letting go will be the best decision ever."
—Author Unknown

THE TRUTH IS A DIFFICULT PILL TO SWALLOW. It takes grit and courage to be *honest* with yourself about your situation, no matter how painful that reality is. I'll give you an example.

When I was married, I wasn't happy. We had gone to counseling three times over a period of three years. Things would get better for six months; then we would go back to the same behaviors that had gotten our relationship in trouble.

I was avoiding the reality that divorce was the solution. I am a product of a divorced family, and I said I would never divorce. I felt like I was going to FAIL at something, anything, in my life, because I would be from a divorced family.

I feared that I'd failed just as my parents did.

There still is a bit of stigma surrounding divorce. It took me the longest time to make peace with what I knew to be inevitable. I went to my pastor, and as I talked to him, he noticed that when we were at church functions, my ex would choose not to be next to our family, or he would sit across the room while other couples would sit and hold hands.

He talked to me and asked what was going on. I said, *"He's an alcoholic. We went to counseling, but it did not get better."* He asked me, *"Why are you still in the marriage?"* I said, *"Well for the kids!"* Then he said, *"Sometimes you can't stay for kids; that's just an excuse!"*

My reaction was *"WHAT??"* He said, *"Your kids can see you are not happy. And consider that kids are affected worse because when they see their parents in an unhappy relationship, it communicates to them it is okay to stay in their own relationships where they may be unhappy."*

The turning point came when my 10-year-old said, *"You should just divorce dad."* We were sitting at the dinner table, and I remember we weren't even talking about his dad at the time. He just blurted it out. My first reaction was *why would he say this?* Then I felt devastation and a sick feeling in my stomach. My mind raced, and I thought *what has he seen or heard to make him come to that conclusion?* But I knew why he said it. My son was a very perceptive child, and he could sense my unhappiness and knew the source. What I couldn't believe was how he even knew or understood what divorce was. This made me sad.

Ultimately the kids were angry at both of us. But I never said anything bad about their dad, and let the kids figure out their relationship with him in their teens. Our divorce was better for everyone. My kids eventually came to the realization of the kind of relationship they could have with their father, and it wasn't me who told them. They figured it out because their dad is still an alcoholic. My son is older now with a child of his own and to this day says, *"I just don't get it!"*

Before we got divorced, I chose to move out. When I approached my ex and said, *"I think we should try to separate, and here's why."* It was one of the hardest conversations I'd ever had with anyone because it broke his heart. He didn't understand why I was doing what I was doing.

The problem was he was an alcoholic and controlling. So much so, I couldn't see it and how it affected me until I started talking to other people about getting divorced. Once I started discussing my decision, almost everyone said, *"Gosh, we are so glad!"* Or, they would say things like: *"Yeah, we didn't like how he treated you, but we thought you were happy!"*

I realized how controlling he had become when he moved us to Arizona and dictated my circle of friends when we lived there. I became a stay-at-home mom, and this isolated me even more. Then he became verbally abusive. I might tell him something like, *"You talk about yourself all the time, and you need to listen because other people want to talk, too."* He would reply, *"Well, Karen, everyone thinks you are a bitch."* And when he said that, he really made me think it was my issue. He would also tell me I didn't remember events in our lives correctly. For example, when I would state he had never told me a particular thing, he would tell me, *"Maybe you are getting sick like your mom, and you aren't remembering things."* It got to the point that I actually started believing what he said.

Through the marriage, I became so ISOLATED that I AL-LOWED him to control me. That's the stuff you don't see when you are in a relationship like that. And when you are so deeply engrossed, you will start to believe what the other person says about you. You think you *are* getting sick. Maybe you *are* someone people don't like. You become what that person says you are.

After I moved out, I started working a job in Phoenix. I would drop the kids at child care, work from 8:30am till 3:30pm and then pick them up at 5:30pm. I wanted to create a stable environment for my kids, and I needed the money. So, I took the military gig in Phoenix, even if it meant I had to drive a lot and do all the parenting things by myself. I wanted to reclaim my independence and not rely on my ex or his income. I wanted to do what I wanted to do for myself. My ex never wanted me to get commissioned or to further my education, but now was the time to show what I could do.

What I learned through all of my newfound independence is it's also important to reach out for help instead of trying to do everything alone. It's hard to see the ugly truth of situations when you're in them. Other people might think you are happy, so they don't interfere in your life with their opinions. The tendency (especially for women in my experience) is to do what has to be done on our own. You might think people don't want to help you, but they do. When I had my hip surgery, people offered to bring food, and I said, *"My dad is coming here,"* as a way to refuse their good intentions. Then I started thinking *NO, these people want to help me, or they wouldn't offer.* So, I had to allow people to bring me food, drop things off, and help me out. I learned they enjoyed doing it as well.

Change was on the horizon in my personal life and for the women in the 1960s, too. (When have we not been in a state of change?) The 1960s, commonly called *"A decade of change for women,"* saw the rise in women in the workplace, and this highlighted the gender pay gap. Sexual harassment was a hot topic, and a record 80% of women used birth control. More women in the workplace brought greater visibility to the problem of the gender pay gap. According to *US News*[3], *"Gradually, Americans came to accept some of the basic goals of the Sixties feminists: equal pay for equal work, an end to domestic violence, curtailment of severe limits on women in managerial jobs, an end to sexual harassment, and sharing of responsibility for housework and child rearing.*" As an apt anthem for the times, Lesley Gore's song, *"You Don't Own Me"* blared from women's stereos.

I understand, Lesley.

Groundbreaking acts and amendments made history, too, including the 1963 Equal Pay Act, 1964 Civil Rights Act, 1972 Title IX of the Education Amendments, and the 1979 Pregnancy Discrimination Act.

The National Organization for Women was established in 1966, and *Ms. Magazine* hit the stands. An increase in women applying for higher paying jobs formerly only available to men trended. Due to medical and workplace advancement, women found they could make broader choices. Getting pregnant didn't mean slamming the brakes on your career. More women attended professional schools and worked outside the home. Women Work Life[4] states the statistics rose in favor of women working more with 27% in 1960 in the workplace to 54% in 1980 to 70% in 2012 and 71.1% in 2018.[5]

When I was in aerospace, my mentor was a senior project manager. I needed his help because I had been transplanted into an environment where people had worked together for a long time. Some of the engineers were doing project management work, some construction managers were doing project management work, and some project managers were managing projects as well. When the senior project manager came on to the job, he separated project management, engineering, and construction management into their own areas. This was a new shift in the way the business would be run. I needed help because a female engineer, who was also doing project management work, had that part of her job taken away and assigned to me. I asked my mentor for help on how to approach her, and how to get her to do what I needed her to do without stepping on her toes. She didn't particularly care for me and treated me badly. I know this because she didn't treat any of the male project managers this way, even though some of them took over a few of her projects. The male project managers felt bad for me and the poor way she treated me, and sadly, she is an example of the way women hold other women back. I lived this, and I know when we do nothing that we allow the type of environment to exist where women can't support women. It was crazy that I had to endure her childish treatment, like ignoring me when I spoke to her, but the problem had to be resolved. I needed to be able to go to work and enjoy my day. Peer pressure from the male project managers, whose attention she enjoyed, didn't seem to move the needle much on her reluctance to work with me.

My mentor said I needed to ask her for the furniture information I needed for the project I had taken over from her and that I should put a deadline to it. As part of a project, she had met with the customer, gotten their furniture layout requirements and then had engineered the area the furniture was to go into. She had also gotten quotes on the furniture build out, worked with the furniture company on what kind of pieces would best go with each other, and put a timeline to the entire process. Then I came in and took over the project management on the entire job. I didn't want to re-do what she'd done; I just wanted her to share her contact information and drawings on the furniture build out. But, she didn't want to be helpful, and it was hard to get information out of her about the vendor she had been working with, the timeline, etc. so I could log it in the project management tracking software.

I was advised to be kind to her, not demanding, and to ask her for input. I was told to make her feel special. I thought doing these things was a waste of time, but that approach did end up being helpful in this instance. She was able to see I wasn't re-doing what she had done with the furniture build. It was so simple. I merely wanted to put the furniture information into the project management software, so I could track the progress of the project. When you are a project manager, you provide a project management plan (PMP), and you use software to schedule the entire project. You insert a timeline and schedule into the software for the different parts of a project to help keep it on track.

My mentor's advice worked for that previous instance. But overall, she was hard to work with. I think it was because she was the only female in the engineering area. Then I came along, a female project manager and all the other male engineers liked me. That didn't sit well with her, and I think she just wanted to hate me. So, I continued to be myself, treat her with respect and was always nice to her. Unfortunately, she continued being nasty. I ignored it. I couldn't change her. I didn't want her friendship. I simply wanted a civil dynamic between us. My mentor's initial advice got the job done because I was able to complete my responsibilities, but that was the extent of it. His advice did nothing to help to heal the rifts in our relationship, and I can't help but think that a woman mentor would have handled this challenge differently. Women are all about relationships. I can just imagine a woman mentor sitting there between two other women who aren't getting along and what she would say. *"Let's dig into this. Are you doing something that bugs her, Karen?"* It's too bad that that wasn't my experience because I have a feeling that I would have come away from that situation far happier and with greater closure.

When you look for a mentor or coach, don't just take anybody on. I personally look for someone who is further along in whatever profession they're in. In my example, my mentor had been a project manager for a long time, and he was a successful leader, so I wanted someone who could articulate success to me.

Also, when you choose a mentor, make sure you get along with their personality. They may have to say harsh things, and it is your job not to get mad about it. I know my mentors need to push me to believe in what I do, whether I believe I can do it or not.

Choosing a mentor who resonates with you can help you to face the truths about your business and life, and while this can be a scary prospect; it is a healthy one. Sometimes, we avoid what we know we need to do because it feels easier to mask the truth than to confront it. I have found that examining what triggers me is an accurate way of tapping into what I need to tackle in my life. It's difficult to make this mindset switch, but we can re-train ourselves to be less fearful and more deliberate about the decisions that we make and the healing that inevitably will accompany us facing our fears.

It is easy to get buried in the day-to-day and to only surface when we are exhausted. As women, we are notorious for this! We are absolutely engulfed in child care, our romantic relationships, our responsibilities as daughters, etc. Add business owner to the mix, and it's *"See you next year!"* But we owe it to ourselves to be mindful, in the moment and present as much as we can be. Life is not just about living in a numb rush, but we are here to grow and improve our experience and ourselves. And how can you immerse yourself in your purpose if you are not able to pick your nose up from the grindstone?

I heard a saying once; it went something along the lines of *"You should try to meditate for 10 hours a day. If you have no time, meditate for an hour."* I don't know who said it, but I think they were on point.

You owe it to yourself to learn the truth about yourself and what you need in your business and life, and as someone who has been there and looked the truth dead in the eye, I also want to tell you that it's not as scary as the scenarios we build up in our minds! Through my life, I have met people who have been sick and had no diagnosis. It was only after they received the diagnosis that they could get started on the path to healing.

I want to also add, that as women we have a responsibility to know and handle the truth. Our fight in the working world and society, in general, isn't over. In fact, it's a way off yet. If we put our heads in the sand, we can't advance our cause together. We can't make progress. Feel the courage of your foresisters and use it to propel you to make changes in your life and to stand in your truth.

Molly, another woman I interviewed, is a whip at making changes in her own life and in helping other young women do the same. She described the positive dynamic in mentoring relationships, sharing that her business is all about mentoring others to run their own cosmetic franchise and/or be a part of her team. She gets to know her mentees by having them describe their "why" of getting into business. Was it for money, success, more time with family, travel, or incentives? Would it surprise you to know the answer doesn't really matter? What mattered was that the recipe for success was the same no matter the "why." Molly teaches that you have to learn the good with the bad and that you are a business person first, and in her case, an artist second. It's not the other way around.

YOUR TO DO:

Find someone who can be your mentor and make formal arrangements. That means setting up a call, talking about how you can both work together, and agreeing on a set of activities going forward.

I typically offer a *free* strategy session to start, so my potential clients and I can decide if we are the right fit for one another. You can make a similar request and arrangement for your first meeting with your potential mentor.

If you'd like, I'd like to give that gift to you as well. Here's how to book your Free Discovery Call: www.WomanOnTop.biz/apply

CHAPTER 5

A Target That Only You Can Hit: Setting And Achieving Goals

"If you don't know where you are going,
any road will get you there."
—Alice In Wonderland

T HERE ARE COMMON MISPERCEPTIONS that it's hard to declare a goal, to reach a goal, or that goals are not important… These assumptions are not true.

My parents taught me to set goals, and so did my teachers in school. They were the "set it, and you can achieve it" type. My father started out as an EMT in the Air Force and then went to school, after I was born, to be an engineer. My mother went to college to be a nurse, through the ROTC program, and then served four years in the Air Force to pay for her college tuition. My goals were to be the best flute player in high school, be the first to go to college in my family, to join the Air Force and eventually end up a commissioned officer. I defined my goals by looking at what I wanted to do in life then I looked at my family and how my going after those goals might affect them, and then I set out to achieve them.

To properly set a goal, you need to write it down, map out the preliminary steps and then envision the goal daily through meditation...keeping only the end in mind without getting enmeshed in the "how's." I now do 5-year vision boards to help with my process of goal setting.

There are a couple of ways to create a vision board. You can either buy a kit or do it yourself. The first one I created was when I was a distributor for a health and wellness company. I attended an event called Human Beings More for Self-Development. The company believes in the five pillars of health, body, mind, family, society, and finances. At this event, you created a vision board that was mapped to these five areas.

The vision board looked something like this:

• Body	• Run a 5K
• Mind	• Attend active listener workshop
• Family	• Re-establish date nights
• Society	• Volunteer at Nepal charity
• Finances	• Save $10K to reinvest into business

The pillars were listed on the left side of the poster paper. And, on the right side, you were instructed to use magazines to cut out pictures, and words, and phrases to help depict the goals in those areas. Then you would glue these pictures, words, and phrases onto the poster board. The design was done this way because it was easy. However, you can certainly use your imagination to customize your board.

I will describe how my vision board looked to give you a better idea of the end goal: For the Body pillar, my vision board had a picture of a woman in her 50s, working out and looking physically fit. It also contained the words "health" and "fitness" as I wanted to get back into shape. For the Mind pillar, I had pictures of self-help books and another diploma as I wanted to better myself and go back to school. For the Family pillar, I had a picture of a woman with two kids eating at a table. I also had a picture of a ring, as I was looking for a healthy relationship(s) for me and my kids. For the Society pillar, I had names and pictures of non-profits, as I wanted to give back. For the Finances pillar, I had a picture of a Mercedes and two houses as I wanted to create enough wealth to afford these things.

When designing a vision board, however you do it, just make sure it is littered with *what* you want in your life. The questions you need to answer are: *What is your goal? Is your goal realistic? Does it fit in with your overall life objectives? Does it make you happy?*

The reason you focus on what you want is because what you focus on happens. Only then you can concentrate on *how* to make it happen. The how is just as important as the what, but most people get caught up in how to do something before they even know what they want.

For example, let's say you have a house on your vision board. Ask yourself: *how will I obtain this house?* First, you will need to go to a mortgage broker. With their help, you will figure out how much you can afford. Then, if all goes according to plan, you will be pre-qualified for a set amount. Using this method, from the get-go, you can start looking at houses in your price range. You won't waste time browsing houses you cannot afford. And, once you find the house you want, you'll simply show the pre-qualification letter to a selling agent. Handling the process this way puts you in the running to buy that perfect house a lot faster. *Or,* you could go about this process completely backward and just shop for houses before being pre-qualified. Doing it this way, you might find the house you love, but can you afford it? Or, you might have to come up with a bigger down payment. And *then* you have to solve how you will make the money you need. This is what I mean by the "how."

Once you've nailed down how you want to manage your goal's process, you can engineer WHEN it is realistic to go after it. Yes, envision it; but don't get too wrapped up in HOW it is going to happen for now. Just make sure the goals are realistic for the timeline; If you have a $20,000 a year job, and you expect to be a millionaire by the end of the year, that's probably not realistic. With my first vision board it took five years to realize most of my goals, but some I still have not obtained. When you do obtain your goals, make another vision board and add new desires to the old.

One of the women interviewed for this book shared her story about creating a vision (board):

"I had a picture on my refrigerator for 16 years. It was one of those old drawings of the houses in the newspaper that you saw, those black and white drawings of a design. So, that picture of the house (that I had) on my refrigerator for 16 years...I live in that house now."

Another example to show that visioning really does work took place in the summer of 2002, when a friend and I decided we wanted to start running. We thought we should run the Rock and Roll half-marathon in Phoenix, Arizona. And we even bought the book for people who hate to run: *The Book of How to Run for Non-Runners*. We looked at the plan, then reverse-engineered how much training we needed to do, to meet our marathon goal in January of 2003. Our training started in June. Meaning, we had six months to reach our goal. We started with running one mile, then two, and then built up to a 5km run, then a 10km, and so on. Through that book, we were taught how to build up to running those milestones, but we had less time than most. Most people who train for a half-marathon actually run a half-marathon distance (13.1 miles) at least once before they go to the final event. We didn't. We trained to a total of nine miles, so stretching to 13.1 miles was pretty hard. However, we were both able to finish and do fairly well in our age brackets.

Setting goals, planning, and taking action with visioning also helps you understand more about your strengths and talents. I got clear about my talents as I progressed in my career in the Air Force and a few of my initial civilian jobs. I found I was good at customer service, and I was good at relating to people. I was good at teaching, and I was good at recognizing what other people's talents are and then helping them to find a job or career that cultivated those talents. I also found I was good at managing projects from start to finish and it was fun! I developed my talents by being in customer service jobs, working on a degree in Organizational Management and then earning my MBA in Project Management.

You have to do what you tend to excel at naturally. If you always feel like you're working and trudging along but not getting anywhere, then what you are doing is probably not the right fit. For example, I started out as an electronic mechanic in the Air Force; I chose that field because I knew it was something that I could do based on my test scores. I also knew it might come in handy down the road in life because I was pursuing a degree in Computer Science. However, I found I struggled at troubleshooting and diagnosing; I could do those types of tasks, but they took a lot of effort. I also found that programming was not something I wanted to do because it didn't involve being with people and it took A LOT of math skills, of which I also was good at, but it didn't excite me.

Another key takeaway from this chapter is to challenge the norm in setting your goals. An example might be retiring at age 65. Who came up with that number anyway? Well, in 1883, the German chancellor, Otto Von Bismarck, in a maneuver against the Marxists who were burgeoning in power and popularity, announced that anyone over 65 years old would be forced to retire and that he would pay a pension to them. Years later the U.S. followed suit with this philosophy[6]. But, who says you can't retire when you are 55 or 45? So, when setting goals, challenge those norms. Just remember to be realistic; if you retire earlier than 65, you may need to cover 25-45 years of income, with some other source. But even as you are realistic, don't *block* yourself from possibility.

Challenge what you think you must have, versus what you actually want. You might recall the magic wand question to help you narrow or broaden your goals. Think: what do you want your life to look like in 5, 10 or 15 years? Get lost in an idea of what you want your life to look like, but don't get stuck or hung-up in the "how," until you define it.

Speaking of getting un-stuck, women kept fighting for their work rights in the 1970s, and the media at this time was known for doing exactly the opposite of what every woman needed: not covering the major stories celebrating women's lib progress. Women Work Life[7] gives us a possible reason why:

"Perhaps this absence was due in part to the dramatic presidential events unfolding in 1973 and 1974, including Watergate, Nixon's resignation, and Ford stepping up as President."

Another win for women came in the form of a Supreme Court Ruling in 1973 prohibiting sex-segregated help wanted ads. A skim through this era of ads reveals one that touts: *"Our Thursday Food Guide is for you. Because you're the smartest homemaker around."* Gag.

I definitely will not be putting that advertisement on my vision board! And I am definitely glad we are not as stuck as we used to be!

YOUR TO DO:

Using the steps outlined above, use a kit, or browse the website below, to create a vision board. Place it somewhere visible and where you will see it *every day*.

This link gives you great starting instructions for making your own vision board. You will learn what materials you need for your board and where you can find pictures (the answer: everywhere)!

https://www.jackcanfield.com/blog/how-to-create-an-empower-ing-vision-book/

Vision boards help women (and men) to manifest and more deeply dissect their goals. You can use vision boards to assist you in nailing your goals, and they are a wonderful visual reminder to stay on track until you attain what you have envisioned.

I think of vision boards as a tangible representation of what athletes do on the regular. They train not only their bodies, but their minds to see the victory. To picture themselves putting on the coveted ring, to see themselves dashing across the line, or the ball flying into the stands or the impossible-seeming leap as they slam the basket from a miracle location on the court.

If you need more motivation to get moving, read the next section, which describes the interview that I had with a force to be reckoned with: Heather.

Since she was a little girl, Heather always wanted to be a leader. She took that drive and created a vision for her current practice as she mapped out a plan. To help with that vision, she asked successful people how they got where they were today. Her goal: she wanted to have 100 clients and $100M in assets.

She didn't make it complicated; her goal was to bring in $2M per month, build relationships and average one referral a day. Then, she kept a sticky note on her computer screen of how much she wanted to make in fee-based assets. That's it! By taking these uncomplicated actions and remaining consistent in her vision, she didn't get stuck. Instead, she hit six figures by year three and is working on seven figures now.

Once she reached her six-figure goal, she set more goals and took notes along the way of where she wanted to be in 10 years. And, every morning, she went through three exercises: 1) what I am grateful for, 2) spend some time with God, 3) set the intention for the day (usually not more than 4).

At the end of the day, she asked herself *"Did I do everything I wanted?"* If she made those intentions happen, then she had a good day. But she doesn't beat herself up if she doesn't make all of the intentions anyway. Chastisement is not the purpose of this exercise. Strategic and steady wins the race is. If she misses the mark, she just moves her intentions to the next day and adds more.

She treats success as more of a hobby than a doing, and all she knows how to do is make it work. Her philosophy: *"I don't have successful or unsuccessful days—I just have days where I have plotted out what I need to do, like call these three clients about XYZ, or it can be as detailed as I want to secure another $10M in advisory."*

Climb the ladder with Heather by getting your *Woman on Top Workbook* here: www.WomanOnTop.biz/bonus

CHAPTER 6

Getting Down To The Bottom Line

"Money is only a tool. It will take you wherever you wish, but it will not replace you as the driver."
—Ayn Rand

ONE OF MY FIRST woman-owned business professional clients thought they didn't have any money left in their budget to save or they needed a minimum amount of money to get started. This particular client continued to grow debt by charging up credit cards with frivolous purchases (buying clothes, going on trips her family couldn't afford, going out to eat all of the time). She would rack up the bills, pay it off with her tax return and then do it all over again.

Ultimately, she wanted to travel and live comfortably (not paycheck to paycheck), and she hoped to run a successful business.

This is what she needed to do to achieve that:

- Change her mindset
- Start saving in small amounts and increase savings quarterly
- Grow her portfolio and use it strictly for retirement

- Put the savings in her business plan. The saying is *"If you don't include it in your plan, it will never get done!"*

One mistruth that often holds people back is the belief that you have to have a lot of money to start investing. Most people think that they cannot save and that they cannot get out of debt. They might feel that they have to put all their cash into the business. I get asked all the time *"What is enough money to retire? My answer is always:* "It depends."

Each person is unique and your goal for anything, whether you are opening a business or planning your retirement, depends on how much you want to spend and how much you have saved. One client of mine has less than $100K saved, but due to her spend rate, she will end up with enough for HER to retire comfortably. Another client who is the same age has $300K saved but will NOT have enough to retire unless he saves more, or chooses to spend less in his retirement.

You must learn how to make money work for you. If you are in debt, list out all of your debt, both the monthly payment and the amount owed. Then divide those numbers to find out how many months it will be until you can pay that debt off. Start with the debt that has the most remaining months until the bill will be paid in full. Plan to pay more against that bill and make minimum payments on all the rest. Once your first bill is paid off, take what you paid on that debt and add it to the next longest payment, until that debt is paid off. Then just keep going down your line of bills until you have paid off every cent you owe.

As a business owner, besides having a business plan and making money work for you, it is important to consult both a tax advisor and a legal advisor. Business owners have unique tax incentives they can cultivate, and, they need to make sure their business is set up the right way (LLC, S-Corp, etc.). As your business grows you may need to change the way your business is structured, and this will also determine your tax incentives.

	L18		f_x							
	A	B	C	D	E	F	G	H	I	J
1	Debt Name	Pay Off	AMP (Average Monthly Payment)	Payoff/AMP	Pay Plan (Lowest to Highest)	Snowball	Months to Pay off			
2										
3	Visa	3000	150	20	2	Pay $375	8			
4	Discover	5000	175	28	3	Pay $550	9			
5	Chase	2000	200	10	1	Pay $225	8			
6										
7										
8	Track what you Make, Spend and Keep; find extra $$ and add to 1st PP (ex. Pay $200+$25 extra from budget)									
9	After paying off the Chase (PP#1), use $225 from that debt + $150 paying on Visa (PP#2) and start paying $375 on Visa									
10	Repeat above process until all debt is paid off; pay down the card you owe the LEAST amount on first so you can see a WIN									
11										

Here are some guidelines for running your own business:

Know your ideal client; if you know your client, you can target market and not waste energy and dollars on trying to build your brand awareness with everyone. Market to a niche and if necessary develop a micro-niche.

Charge what you are worth; remember time = $$, so you have to figure out what your hourly rate is, then multiply the number of hours it will take to do whatever task you are charging for. Increase your rates if you need to!

You can start by finding out what your expenses are, so you can decide what income you need to sustain that debt, plus make a profit. Also, don't do stuff you suck at! Again, time is money! If it takes you longer to do something, then hire it out.

Increase the percentage going into your 401(k), SEP or SIM-PLE plan; start small and each year increase it until you reach the max for your age group.

Put a percentage of your paycheck in savings; use this for an emergency fund. (You should ultimately have 3-12 months of savings to cover expenses in case something happens, and you cannot work. Start small and increase every month, every quarter, or every time you get a raise.

Here's a little inspiration for you in the form of a woman who has budgeted successfully to reach her goals:

<u>If Dawn can do it, *you* can do it!</u>

- She started a safety training Company
- She and her husband choose to make six figures
- She speaks all over the country and trains speakers
- She has been self-employed for 25 years
- She established her business in a mostly male-dominated field
- She priced her services higher than the Red Cross, and other competitors for strategic reasons.

YOUR TO DO:

Set up a budget. Track all expenses and income. Stay true to this budget for six months and then evaluate where you are.

<u>A simple budget should include:</u>

- Income
- Expenses
- Tracking how close you are to reaching your goal. If your budget totals out to negative numbers, then you have to figure out where to cut your expenses, so you can run your business (and your life) in the black.

YOUR OTHER TO DO...KNOW YOUR HISTORY...SO YOU CAN APPRECIATE YOUR OPPORTUNITIES

According to the National Office of Statistics[8], "...the office of the 80s was much more male-dominated. In 1985 men filled two million more jobs than women. By June 2005, the ratio was much closer to 50:50. This feminization of the workplace is due primarily to the increase in part-time employment."

This age of no technology meant stress levels weren't as high as they are today. People were able to get away from the constant barrage of pings and dings. Relationships were cultivated and nurtured even in the workplace because people paid attention to each other and looked each other in the eye when they spoke. Can you imagine? Issues rarely reached the breaking point because people took time to talk out their problems.

Let's make her-story together! Book your FREE Discovery Call with me here: www.WomanOnTop.biz/apply

CHAPTER 7:

The Power In Failure

*"Just because you fail once doesn't mean you're
gonna fail at everything."*
—Marilyn Monroe

L ET'S TALK ABOUT THIS BOOK. It was one of the projects I had on my bucket list. I wrote it to deliver value to the market and promote my offering. To reverse-engineer the objectives into actionable steps, I met with a publisher and set out a time schedule.

The publisher and I talked through the steps, and I followed examples on his website for what to do; he has a proven process to get published and a managed project schedule. This is based on other book writers and books he has published.

I was going along great, figuring out my content; coming up with examples and fleshing out what I wanted to say, and just when I was close to finishing, I got stopped by compliance. I had received permission to write my book but was never told that I had to actually finish the manuscript before I started to promote it. I paid for a URL and had a website set up but was told the website was not approved by compliance and that I had to shut it down. So, I not only shut down everything; I let that one event define how and when I was to move forward. The coach I was using had a proven process, and I was not able to follow it, so I thought I had to quit everything, including WRITING the book.

Even though I had a hiccup in the process, I was able to meet with my publisher and get back on track; and even though I couldn't follow the process, I could modify it to fit my needs and still get my book done. You can apply this principle to anything you want to achieve.

For example, let's say you declare your goal as follows:

"I want to quit my job in the next 10 years, buy a new home in five years and travel to a new exotic location in the world every six months.
(Business Owner)*"*

Start with the furthest or largest goal first, then add additional goals.

Quit job – 10 yr.	$500,000
Buy house – 2 yr.	$100,000
Travel – 6 months	$5000

Create the budget; then start saving for the nearest goal. Roll off each goal as it is met. Add the $$ from the first goal to the next goal; which will accelerate meeting the furthest or largest goal.

Contrast this with goal-setting in the 1990s, and you can surely see the difference between how women would handle tackling their dreams then and now.

Thank goodness we have actionable steps we can take now, and that we are even permitted to dream of taking steps.

But I digress.

The biggest difference the 1990s brought about was that *both* women and men were willing to make tradeoffs in their jobs to allow for more flexibility in dependent care. And even though men and women were both working and burning the candle at both ends, women were still expected to uphold their domestic duties. *The New York Times*[9] conducted a survey and reported: *"This is true even in families where women contribute half or more of the family income, and where workers are young."*

Additionally:

"*Younger workers are no more likely to be personally prepared to work in a racially and technically diverse environment than older workers.

"*Men and women of color and white women view the chances of advancement for white men as higher than do white men.

"*Workers see little difference between male and female managers. However, managers, male or female, with childcare responsibilities are seen as more sympathetic to employees with family-related conflicts. 'A good manager can stand in the worker's shoes and in the manager's shoes and come up with a solution... This conflicts with the stereotype that people with kids will be too consumed to do a good job.'

"*Conflicts between work and family tend to be resolved in favor of the job, usually to the detriment of the family and the worker...

"Faith Wohl, director of human resource initiatives at Du Pont, said, *'I still think it's a problem of productivity. But the workplace itself may be the problem. It may be intensifying the fragility of the family. The worker brings an additional set of problems back into the workplace."*

It's surprising to note that employees who had switched jobs in the last five years rated low salary and benefits in the bottom portion of the 20 reasons they chose to relocate. People wanted jobs that encouraged open communication and the flexibility for their families. A mere 35% of people polled in this survey ranked salary as the most important incentive to change jobs.

The article ends with a bit of foreshadowing that we can appreciate all these decades later, which confirms that while the work may change in scope and application, the needs of the people, and particularly those with children never do: "…workers really do want more control over their destiny and, up to a point, will sacrifice cash to get it."

Many people were taking action to begin to even-out what would be known as "work/life balance." But they didn't have a plan.

You do!

YOUR TO DO:

Even though you may not be able to follow a set process to get something accomplished, it doesn't mean failure. What goal has been put on the back burner due to an obstacle? What could be modified or changed to get you back on track to meet that goal?

Write out your monetary goals and then set realistic budgets against the goals.

Use the *Woman on Top Workbook* to help you implement what you learn in this book.

Here's your link: www.WomanOnTop.biz/bonus

CHAPTER 8:

Getting Out Of Your Way And The Art Of Delegation

"Deciding what not to do is as important as deciding what to do."
—Jessica Jackley

W HEN I WORKED IN AEROSPACE, a colleague of mine wanted to set up safety standards around hearing protection. During the project she couldn't let go of the administrative tasks; she was not delegating, and she was doing too much of the work assigned to other teammates.

Even after being coached, she continued to try to take on *all* the items of the project even though it was split between three people. This caused internal conflicts amongst the team. Her decision to continue to do all the work started to derail the project. Team members didn't feel valued, and they felt their contribution didn't matter. She should have focused on her part of the project, and allowed management to help with the personnel issues so that all the tasks could be done in a timely manner.

Often, people misunderstand delegation. They don't realize that it is okay to let some tasks be completed by others. You don't have to handle all the aspects of the project yourself. Delegation is showing trust in another, and you have to understand that people arrive at answers in different manners and time. However, they will ultimately arrive at the same answer(s) you may have. Or, they may come up with a better solution. You must trust the process. Don't micromanage because it kills creativity.

For example, I know my time is priceless, so I only work on what I am good at, and I delegate the rest. It takes less time and effort. I track the milestones to the goal, and then break it down into trimester/monthly/daily tasks. Each person on the team has their part to do because they do it well. This is the best and most efficient way to get things done.

In project management, there is a model of constraints used consisting of cost, scope and time (often called a schedule). It is sometimes referred to as the project management triangle. If one part of the triangle gets out of whack, it can affect the other parts and make the triangle lopsided.

1. Quick and high quality = High cost
2. Quick and low cost = Not high quality
3. High quality and low cost = Takes more time

When you view your business through the lens of project management, it is easy to understand how delegation works and how it can help your business. Again, to reiterate time is precious to me. Since it is, I may have to pay more to get quality, quick turn around on projects I farm out. But it is worth it to me!

And while I have only reinforced my belief that my time is priceless, countless women in the early 2000s preceded me.

Another *New York Times*[10] article I found while doing research painted a picture of what was happening to girl power, stating that *"Up until the late 1990s, the United States stood out among developed countries for its higher female labor force participation rate. But that's when other countries started to catch up."*

The United States saw the female labor force diminish without recovering since the first time those original pioneering women set foot on the line.

The news wasn't all discouraging, however. Women outpaced men in getting their bachelor's degrees, which closed up more of the gender gap in the workplace. But there was still work to do (because isn't there always, sisters?) In a poll taken of married people, it was found that men made more money and more quickly at that! A short leap can be made to the assumption (fact) that women would have felt discouraged and thought *what's the point of leaving the house?*

We haven't made much more traction since then, which is unfortunate… But hey, we will continue the fight, and we will reach fair and equal treatment in the workplace, where we can delegate to our heart's content!

YOUR TO DO:

Practice delegating just ONE thing in your business or personal life to someone else and see how much time it frees up for you to do other jobs (or the job you are the best at).

For example, hire someone to do billing or social media for your company. Even though you may like doing these types of tasks; time = money. If your hourly rate is $50/hr and it takes you 2 hours to do a task, isn't it worth it to hire someone for $15/hr to do it in 1 hour?

Among women, there seems to be a common thread of thought… **We often believe we are responsible for everything and everyone.**

Why wouldn't we feel this way? Since the dawn of time when we were raising our children in caves and preparing mammoth for dinner, we have been conditioned to do more gathering than hunting, to "keep the home fires burning." That's all well and good, but our history also makes us vulnerable to being control freaks.

It might feel downright alien to you not to be in charge of bringing the soccer team's snacks, of not managing paying the bills, of handing over the household duties to someone else (no matter how much we might dream of a personal chef or housekeeper). So, we do not naturally gravitate toward delegation, but just because that seems to be the truth for most women, doesn't mean a habit, even an instinct can't be unlearned. It also doesn't mean we can't condition ourselves to detach emotion from our professional duties.

When you run your own business, emotion and strategy are inextricably linked, and it can feel like every decision HAS TO BE emotional or it won't feel authentic.

I am all for authenticity, but I am also all for progress, growth and systematizing business to allow it to scale. When you do this, you are allowing yourself to work to your full potential.

So, what can you delegate first? There's an old saying about delegation that makes a great starting point for deciding what responsibility to let go of. *"Do what you do best and delegate the rest."*

You will probably want to keep in your wheelhouse the tasks that best match your strengths, and likely, these tasks are probably also easier for you to do. You might even enjoy them. This is an excellent sign that you should retain what you can do efficiently and well in-house.

That's not to say you get to keep every easy task. If you love formatting your monthly newsletter for example, but you could pay someone to do the same job, so you could focus elsewhere—where your time and money would be applied to more valuable duties—what do you think is the right decision for you?

A lot of times, the inability to delegate begins with the fact that the person attempting to do so has a hard time trusting people to handle what they normally do. I get it. It's terrifying to think about someone screwing up your accounts, relationships, or finances, but if you don't take the chance on getting help, then you will stay limited by your own bandwidth. You can accomplish more and help more people; you can do what you are supposed to do and shine in your purpose when you delegate. And isn't that the objective? Also, it is AWESOME to strengthen the bonds of trust and deepen relationships with people you depend on. You get to know them; they get to know you, and when everything is in alignment, it's almost intuitive. You don't want to miss out on that!

HERE'S YVETTE'S STORY ABOUT DELEGATION:

Yvette is a restaurant owner with her sister. She bought the restaurant her mother owned, and then later on bought another restaurant

81

across the street. This was back in the day before computers and automation. Meaning, she had to learn the art of delegation fast, and she now considers it a necessity of business ownership. Trust is the biggest part of delegation, and she had to learn to trust those who worked for her. When I talked to her, she agreed the people you appoint might not do the task the way you might do it, but if the end result is good, she is good with it. Ultimately, she didn't want to do the day-to-day anymore, as she didn't want to live at the restaurant. So, she hired great people, and she delegated all the rest!

Let's take a page out of Yvette's book for ourselves.

I've shared a lot of stories with you, but I would love to hear what's going on in your life that I can help you with. **I am passionate about coaching and advising women just like you looking to break out of the confines of the patriarchy in the workplace.**

It's as simple as sending me a private email to get the process rolling. Email me here: womanontopbook@gmail.com

P.S. I can't wait to talk to you!

CHAPTER 9:

You Are Either Growing Or You Are Going

"In order to be irreplaceable, one must always be different."
—CoCo Chanel

L ET'S TALK ABOUT LIFE and business reinvention. I had a client, who had twin boys with ADD. In their cases, nothing traditional worked to help them succeed in life and school. My client found that through applying the lessons she had learned from hypnosis that she was taking for her own personal growth, it helped her sons with their learning and relaxation. She then opened her own practice and used her family's success to alleviate pain and frustration in others.

We all need to continue to grow, but some people possess the belief that you grow just simply by trying. I think there is more to it than that.

Think of it this way: Praising *effort* over *progress* is what many parents have done with their children, and we have an entire generation being rewarded for *mediocrity* versus actual *growth*.

Carol Dweck, a psychologist at Stanford University, explains that parents should explain to children that important goals do exist and then help their kids form a plan to reach the goals, as doing so will advance a child's growth mindset. This same principle can be applied as adults as well.

In my opinion, the way we are handling our children's effort is detrimental to girls especially as they get older. Kids who partake in sports where the scoring is tallied this way are so completely ill-prepared for what they will encounter in the workplace. They haven't sharpened their skills or resolve. They haven't practiced increasing their stamina. They are not prepared to compete. **Winning in earnest helps you identify your special skills and mentally prepares you for using them later in life.**

My daughter played softball, and in her league no matter how well or poorly you played, you would earn a trophy. While this sounds nice and fair in theory, it taught my daughter that she was average. That's what happens when you treat people this way. Especially kids. They stay average. Then, in a sad twist, she began to compare herself to other people in the house, saying *"Everybody is smarter than me."*

When I think back on that time, when inside I was just begging her to believe in herself, I am so glad I am her mom. Because not only was I determined to make waves in my career for me, and other women, I knew my daughter was watching me. She was witnessing me go to work in a field presided over by men and noticing how I stayed put, did my job and let my work speak for itself while also refusing any mistreatment. Thankfully, she came out of that period and found all the tools she needed to compete with her male counterparts successfully.

Conversely, my mother became a nurse because it was one of the only professions she could take at the time. In the meantime, my dad encouraged my brother and me to learn about science. He was enthusiastic about our learning through experimenting. My brother grew up to become a self-taught programmer, and maybe it was his frame of mind that was considered advanced in his time that pushed me to believe I could go toe to toe with any man in any role.

I don't want any of us to be "average" women. We are better than that.

One of the ways that I prepare to meet my male constituents head on is to prepare my mind for the day. You've heard the saying *"Garbage in, garbage out"*? Well, this is maybe even more relevant to the diet we feed our minds.

For my daily rituals (and to remain un-average), I read or watch daily doses of positivity quotes or mindsets to keep me positive and on track with my Vision. I track my daily, monthly and quarterly success and then make minor adjustments to stay congruent. I read daily as well; either about personal growth, positive physical change or new business methods I would like to implement in my business.

We have a responsibility to lead as fearlessly as possible not just for ourselves, but because of our daughters, too. We need to consistently encourage them that the fight is worth it from the sweeping, staggering truth of the #metoo movement to the fact that in 2018 it is newsworthy to note that over 100 women were elected to the House of Representatives. That's more women filling seats than in any other year in *her-story* and history. But a part of me feels this shouldn't have made the news. If we had moved further along to progression, no one would care whose butts were in the seats.

I lead as fearlessly as possible to accommodate for the changes that are happening every day in the businesswoman's world and in our daughters' world.

<u>By 2010, we've made some life-altering-strides:</u>

- Increasing our presence in the workforce. In 1970 30.3 million women were working outside the home and in 2010 women numbered 72.7 million.
- Women making up 37.97% percent of the labor force, and:
  - Expanding the industries in which they are working. We are penetrating specialties like accountancy, law enforcement, litigation, medicine, and pharmacology.
  - The majority of women being employed in these occupations: secretary, administrative assistant, cashier, and elementary and middle school teachers.

However, after everything we have put ourselves through to be heard and to shift the perception of our worth, we still only earned $0.77 to every dollar earned by a man.

Since making such progress and so quickly, understandably the number of women in the workforce has risen more slowly.

<u>Here are the numbers in 2017:</u>

- 74.6 million women are employed outside the home.
- 47% of women are present in the US labor force.

Most excitedly…

The number of businesses that women own have reached nearly 10 million.

The revenue from these women is sky-high at a jaw-dropping $1.4T.

Working moms are no longer the exception to the rule. In fact, 75% of mothers have a full-time job.

40% of households with children under 18 are supported by mothers as the primary earners. That's quite a boost from 1960 when women in the workforce averaged 11% (a paltry representation, ladies).

The number of women with college degrees have quadrupled since 1970.

Women are seen in greater numbers in professional and managerial positions.

The unemployment rate for women has dropped to 4.8%, down over four percentage points from November 2010.[11]

Why did I take you in the Women's Movement time machine as I recounted my own personal experience?

Sometimes, we might get so caught up in our lives that we forget how fortunate we are. We forget pain can be a catalyst into a better life.

But it can be a tricky thing to be a woman. Of course, we are fortunate to be amazing, and beautiful, and intelligent *(and thank God, we don't have a penis)*, but there were times when we were denied our very rights as human beings.

The pasts and presents of women are woven together like a tapestry of time, illustrating the stories of the women we see as some of our strongest role models.

From Amelia Earhart, in the 1930s we learned that just because no women had gone before her to fly a plane, it didn't mean she couldn't do it, or that any one of us can't achieve exactly what we want in our lives.

From Rosie the Riveter, in the 1940s we learned that we can do whatever men do despite the type of job or the perception of others. In the face of a crisis, women kept business doors open, children fed, and bills paid.

From Lena Madesin Phillips, the founder of the Business and Professional Women's Organization in the 1950s, we learned that we accomplish more together and that our sisterhood is a place to feel supported and understood. We should always hold it in the highest honor.

From Eleanor Roosevelt, in the 1960s we learned that we could be seen as people who are worthy of making the same pay as a man when she became the co-head on the Commission on the Status of Women. While we still have work to do in this area, Eleanor ramped up the visibility in this movement through her platform as the First Lady.

From Gloria Steinem, in the 1970s we learned about her vision of gender equality. As taken from her What Would It Be Like If Women Win testimony before the Senate Judiciary Committee:

"In Women's Lib Utopia, there will be free access to good jobs—and decent pay for the bad ones women have been performing all along, including housework. Increased skilled labor might lead to a four-hour workday, and higher wages would encourage further mechanization of repetitive jobs now kept alive by cheap labor… Schools and universities will help to break down traditional sex roles, even when parents will not. Half the teachers will be men, a rarity now at preschool and elementary levels; girls will not necessarily serve cookies or boys hoist up the flag."

We are getting there, Gloria.

From *Working Girl*, in the 1980s we learned that just because you started life without financial advantages, it didn't mean that you weren't as smart or smarter than anyone else even those "above your station." And we discovered that women can be both gorgeous and a genius. The two qualities are not mutually exclusive.

From Madeleine Albright, who became the first female Secretary of State in the 1990s, we learned that political opportunities were not male-exclusive.

From Hillary Clinton, in the 2000s and beyond, we learned that a woman can dream to do anything and then set out to achieve it. Despite losing the election, Hillary still had her share of firsts: she was the first former First Lady to hold a major elective office, and the first woman candidate for presidency to almost be elected from a major political party.[12]

From Michelle Obama, who became the first African American First Lady, we learned that your dreams can come true no matter your ethnicity or sex. A famous quote of hers that every woman can agree with is: *"As women, we must stand up for each other."*[13]

Our road to now has been paved by the fire, hearts, and spirits of the women who preceded us and fought for our future. It's important to remember their missions and struggles as we embrace our missions and share the torch with the crusading women of today.

I met a memorable woman who serves as a brilliant example of the types of support we can and should aspire to be. I had given a speech at a Kiwanis Club, and the talk went over well with both sexes under 60. The older men had an issue with the title of chapter one of this book "You Don't Need a Penis To Succeed," and they even made fun of it to the disdain of one woman, who emailed me apologizing for the men's behavior. I specifically use this language in my talk to get people to sit up and listen. This was a case of men treating women as a threat and the women getting defensive (for good reason). As a woman, who hopes men will read her book, I want men to know that I wish we would focus on solution providing and not tearing each other down because we are trying to make sense of an unfamiliar person, role, adjustment, etc. It makes so much more sense when we engage with each other to reach resolution together.

Continuing to grow, so I can keep alive our female ancestors' legacy, as well as my own, is a big part of my process, and I call myself a life-long learner. It makes me happy. I never was the traditional student. I started my college days when I was 18 but had to take a hiatus due to my mother's sickness. I didn't get back to obtaining my bachelor's degree until I was 22. Then it took me 10 years of going part-time to finally finish. My son was three by then, and I have pictures of him in my graduation ceremony!

I didn't stop there; after I got divorced, I went back to school to get my MBA in Project Management. I graduated Magna Cum Laude, and actually cried when I read the diploma. By then I'd added my daughter to the mix. Both my children experienced me working and going to school full-time. They were very proud of me, and I was thrilled to show them how they can continue to grow.

Of course, you guessed it; I applied and was selected for another MBA program with the aerospace company I worked for. I then received a degree in Supply Chain Leadership and graduated in 2012.

Why do I tell you all of this?

Because I love to learn, and I believe it is a crucial part of my success as an entrepreneur and business owner. I don't think you need several degrees to be successful; my point here is that you need to learn. And keep on learning.

To this day, I read at least four new books per year. Usually either as part of a book club or as part of the Female Empowered Money Maker's (FEMM) Mastermind group. We meet virtually 2x per month; we have an expert talk to us quarterly, and then we meet in person quarterly (usually in the state of one of our members). We also have an App that we track our daily activities on. They are: read goals, exercise, one hour of money making activity, learn (read/audible/YouTube/podcast), and meditate. To have the advantage of other women to bounce ideas off of and to wallow with when we are "in the swamp" is powerful.

Successful people never stop learning and neither should you!

YOUR TO DO:

Pick a self-help book you have been meaning to read and start it.

<u>Here's a list of my favorites:</u>

1. ***Think and Grow Rich for Women***: *Using Your Power to Create Success and Significance* (Sharon Lechter, Sandra Burr). It combines Hill's classic 13 Steps to Success with case studies of noteworthy women.

2. ***Profit First***: *Transform Your Business from a Cash-Eating Monster to a Money Making Machine* (Mike Michalowicz). This book offers a simple, counterintuitive cash management solution that will help small businesses break out of the doom spiral and achieve instant profitability.

3. ***Captivate***: *The Science of Succeeding with People* (Vanessa Van Edwards). Vanessa shares shortcuts, systems, and secrets for taking charge of your interactions at work, at home, and in any social situation. These aren't the people skills you learned in school. This is the first comprehensive, science-backed, real-life manual on how to captivate anyone—and a completely new approach to building connections.

4. ***Mind Over Money Management***: *Strategies Your Financial Advisor Won't Give You* (Robyn Crane). Whether you need help with money management, stress management, or debt consolidation, this book will help you build a solid foundation to better your personal finances forever.

5. ***The Girls' Guide to Building a Million-Dollar Business*** (Susan Wilson Solovic). Susan offers frank advice and hard-won lessons including: taking emotions out of the workplace; making business decisions based on what is best for the company, not on your personal feelings; thinking big and bold; believing that you can be successful and that it is important

93

to be willing to announce your intentions to the world. You'll also learn about managing for growth, and how to hire the right people and discover the best ways to keep them.

Has that list of books (and hopefully this book) gotten you all fired up to claim your life and your purpose? I can help you with those first scary steps of implementing your brand-new business.

Contact me here: www.WomanOnTop.biz/apply

CHAPTER 10:

Bringing It All Together

There's a reason why I wrote this book. It's for all women who struggle, but especially for the women in my circle, like my daughter-in-law who told me the outlandish story of the male bus drivers being hired at higher wages and the fact that these bus drivers sign up for the athletic events and don't volunteer for arts or band competitions. They leave those excursions to the gals.

That instance and other injustices still exist despite the women's movement and staying silent and docile are not what move the needle of progress. So, I will speak out and raise my voice when it's needed to right a wrong, and I know you will do the same. Just like the story of the male bus drivers...yes, in 2018, there are millions of other tales of circumstances where women are enduring being treated as "less than."

Hopefully, this book will coax you into using your own *femme fatale* powers to change this world. Because sister, we need you!

These are the main lessons I hoped to get across to you in the prior chapters, so you can use them to reign over your own life.

Chapter 1 – We delved into the success women have experienced through anecdotes or historical references. This is also where you can get your *Woman on Top Workbook!* Remember these questions I asked you to answer in your journal.

<u>If you haven't done this exercise yet, now is the perfect time!</u>

- Look at your life and compare what you do, versus what you would prefer to do. What would you do if you could be un-compromisingly who you want to be?

- Where in your life are you executing processes a certain way, even though you know there is a better way, but you aren't being listened to when you make suggestions?

- Where in your life are you doing work for someone else, but it's not congruent with who you are?

Chapter 2 – Overcoming perfection is a common obstacle that many women must find the courage to face. Don't forget the statistics that explain how the sense of needing to be perfect is embedded in us. Women have proven that they need to feel 100% confident to go after a job they are interested in, whereas, men only need to feel 60-65% qualified to apply. If you adopted a male mindset when it came to going after what you wanted in your career, how different do you think your life would be? This is also the chapter where I encourage you to go deep into your mind and pull out a goal you have been dreaming of but have been hesitant to embrace. If you haven't yet, don't forget to ask yourself the questions at the end to move you forward toward your goal.

Chapter 3 – Self-care seems to be a big buzzword in 2018, but this year, women are discovering self-care entails more than hopping into a bubble bath. Self-care spans into all areas of your life and speaks of the need to proactively take care of yourself and to make sure that you are kind to yourself when the you-know-what hits the fan. When you think of self-care, think of every area of your life that can benefit from it: personal, a romantic partnership, friendships, your health, and career. But the list doesn't stop there. You can apply the need to care for yourself well to virtually anything! And don't forget that healthy self-care includes setting boundaries in your life.

Chapter 4 – The importance of getting a mentor and the benefits to both mentor and mentee are the main topics of this chapter. This is the place to go if you need help figuring out what to say to a prospective mentor and to learn the difference between a good and poor mentor.

Chapter 5 – We all need a plan when we set our sights on goals. This chapter gives you the tools to plan for what you need to do to achieve your goals. You learned the basics to start on your vision board, and I showed you an example of one I had created. If you need help getting started or a list of possible materials to use, re-visit the link I supplied in this chapter.

Chapter 6 – This chapter is all about your budget, and here, I taught you what a budget is comprised of, and how to back into financial goals as well as provided you with a worksheet to help you build your savings and pay down your debt. By the end of this chapter, you will be able to set and maintain a budget.

Chapter 7 – Failure is actually power if you have the right perspective. We discussed that even though failing is cringeworthy, it also gives you priceless information. Not to mention you checked out a spreadsheet on how to approach your goals, so they have less of a chance of not working.

Chapter 8 – Delegation was the topic, and I shared with you the benefits of delegating, advice on how to begin the delegation process, and even how to learn to trust if you are having issues following through with your delegation goals. We also chatted about why we tend to shy away from delegation…seeing as we are in charge of managing and nurturing everything in the world after all. I also shared with you a method that I use in project management, and that is a simple concept to remember. Called a model of constraints, it consists of cost, scope and time (often called a schedule). It is also sometimes referred to as the project management triangle. Feel free to customize it for your project needs. I think it makes striking a balance a little easier since this is such a visual aid.

Chapter 9 – The main takeaway of this chapter is that whatever you learn, you have the capacity to leverage. Understanding and safeguarding your process of seeking and growing is just as important as any of the other steps in your success plan. We also skipped down the women's movement memory lane to learn once again about the courage of the women who are responsible for our leaps and bounds in the labor force and beyond. Tune into my top five self-health books of all time, too!

Chapter 10 – Here we are!

It is my hope that you will see this book as a guide you can return to time and time again as you steer past the hurdles in your life and leave them in the dust behind you. (Where they belong!)

The fact is, as women, we have an advantage in the workforce. Yes, undoubtedly, we have had our share of battles, but we have made huge progress that we need to be grateful for and continue to advance.

This is why the world needs you. It needs opinions, your voice, your actions, your advocacy, your modeling for the younger generation, your persistence, your belief, your courage, your moxie, your unique brand of womanhood that you present to everyone you meet. When we combine our superpowers together, there isn't anything we can't do, including finally, evening out the gender wage divide.

Men need you, too. They need women to teach them how to treat us. Men are used to the way things have been for as long as they can remember. By and large, they haven't joined us in the marches; they haven't picketed for equal pay and treatment; they haven't protested. Their identities and lives have not been saturated with the subliminal and constant undermining that women have been subjected to. Even the men who try to understand can't, and the rest of them seem worried that if we are given power, we will abuse it, so they squash our outcries with platitudes and one-dimensional and irrelevant arguments.

Besides the influence in our voices, the other massive and priceless weapon women have at their disposal is their belief that the actions we take together will lead to meaningful and monumental change.

Even when you don't want to when you are tired of fighting and correcting and educating and standing in your truth of what must change…

Believe in the power of visualizing the change you wish to see and be in the world.

I can't wait to talk to you about structuring the business you have been longing to launch. Contact me for your Free Discovery call at www.WomanOnTop.biz/apply.

You were meant to be a *Woman On Top!*

Acknowledgments

THERE ARE SO MANY PEOPLE I would like to thank who have supported and encouraged me to get this book done! Thank you so much for your love, kick in the butt when I needed it, and push to finish despite all the curve balls.

Thank you, Ron, my partner, my love, my motivation. You are my rock, and I'm so grateful for your encouragement to keep going when it gets tough. Thank you for putting up with me, even when I am hard to get along with!

Jarod and Jenna, you are so fun to watch as you grow into young adults. I am grateful each and every day that you continue to love and support me. I love you so much. I am blessed to be your mom!

To the book launch team, thank you for taking the time to care; thank you for your thoughts, and thank you for being my biggest cheerleaders! Honest feedback is always the best, and you gave it!

To my coaches: Robyn, Trevor, LoriAnne, Jon, and Hilary. You're an incredible support system of experts. I am so glad to have such an outstanding group of people to work with. But mostly to Hilary who saved my butt at the very end!

To my publisher: Epic Author Publishing. Thank you so much. This book is a 40 year dream come true. Trevor, you made it all possible. Your process works so well. It's such an awesome feeling to finally have this book done.

Finally, to all the women out there who have struggled in male-dominated industries or who have gotten stuck in business. I hope this book has given you the tools and techniques to be a *WOMAN ON TOP!*

References

1. American Express OPEN. "State of Women Owned Business-es Executive Report: Summary of Important Trends, 2007-2016." Women Able. Accessed December 3, 2018. http://www.womenable.com/content/userfiles/2016_State_of_Women-Owned_Businesses_Executive_Report.pdf.

2. Lewis, Jone Johnson. "Slow and Steady: Women's Chang-ing Roles in 1930s America." Thoughtco. Accessed Decem-ber 04, 2018. https://www.thoughtco.com/womens-rights-1930s-4141164.

3. "The 1960s: A Decade of Change for Women." U.S. News & World Report. Accessed December 04, 2018. https://www.usnews.com/news/articles/2010/03/12/the-1960s-a-decade-of-change-for-women.

4. "Women and Work in the 1970s." Women, Work, and Life. August 12, 2014. Accessed December 04, 2018. http://www.womenworklife.com/2014/07/30/work-life-really-like-wom-en-1970s/.

5. "Employment Characteristics of Families - 2017." Bureau of Labor Statistics. Accessed December 3, 2018. https://www.bls.gov/news.release/pdf/famee.pdf.

6. "The New York Times." Wikipedia. December 02, 2018. Ac-cessed December 04, 2018. https://en.wikipedia.org/wiki/The_New_York_Times.

7. "Women and Work in the 1970s." Women, Work, and Life. August 12, 2014. Accessed December 04, 2018. http://www.

womenworklife.com/2014/07/30/work-life-really-like-women-1970s/.

8. "Spotlight on - the 1980s Workplace." Personnel Today. October 23, 2013. Accessed December 04, 2018. https://www.personneltoday.com/hr/spotlight-on-the-1980s-workplace/.

9. Noble, Barbara Presley. "At Work; Dissecting the 90's Workplace." The New York Times. September 19, 1993. Accessed December 04, 2018. https://www.nytimes.com/1993/09/19/business/at-work-dissecting-the-90-s-workplace.html.

10. Covert, Bryce. "The Best Era for Working Women Was 20 Years Ago." The New York Times. September 02, 2017. Accessed December 04, 2018. https://www.nytimes.com/2017/09/02/opinion/sunday/working-women-decline-1990s.html.

11. 11. "Angela Young (not Verified)." 7 Things Companies Can Do to Fight Child Labor | U.S. Department of Labor Blog. Accessed December 04, 2018. https://blog.dol.gov/2017/03/01/12-stats-about-working-women.

12. 12. Lewis, Jone Johnson. "Famous and Powerful Women of the Decade - 2000-2009." Thoughtco. Accessed December 04, 2018. https://www.thoughtco.com/famous-and-powerful-women-of-2000s-4122807.

13. 13. "Dailybreak.com." Dailybreak. Accessed December 04, 2018. https://www.dailybreak.com/break/life-lessons-from-michelle-obama-list.

BOOK BONUS

Download your FREE Woman On Top Workbook.

www.WomanOnTop.biz/bonus

About The Author

KAREN KOENIG HAS OVER 30 YEARS' experience in male-dominated fields. She spent 26 years in the military, six years in aerospace and then changed careers entirely and went into financial services in 2015.

While in the military, Karen rose to the rank of Major and she figured out quickly that you can't command people but learned you can only advise and guide. She then took that experience into the aerospace industry, and not only did she advise and guide, Karen learned it was not about perfection but getting the job done well.

Not wanting to continue in corporate America, Karen then opened a financial services business. There she has learned, (along with her other experiences) that success doesn't mean self-sacrifice and to stand in her power and behind what she believes in.

All these experiences, military, aerospace and financial services have shaped Karen to write this book, so women can know they don't have to take a step back but a step forward into their success.